Religion and the Persistence of Capitalism

RONALD H. PRESTON

RELIGION AND
THE PERSISTENCE OF
CAPITALISM

The Maurice Lectures for 1977
and other studies in
Christianity and Social Change

SCM PRESS LTD

334 02309 2

First published 1979
by SCM Press Ltd
58 Bloomsbury Street, London

Typeset by Gloucester Typesetting Co Ltd
and printed in Great Britain by
Billing & Sons Ltd
Guildford, London and Worcester

Contents

Preface

To choose the title 'Religion and the Persistence of Capitalism' for the Maurice Lectures of 1977 is deliberately to set them in the context of a Christian debate on capitalism which was inaugurated half a century ago by R. H. Tawney's *Religion and the Rise of Capitalism*, and continued a quarter of a century later by V. A. Demant's *Religion and the Decline of Capitalism*. Tawney's book became a classic of twentieth-century British historical writing, its sales running into six figures, and its translations into seven languages. It is a bold and perhaps foolhardy decision to continue the debate after another quarter of a century, and that for at least two reasons. The first is that Tawney's task was simpler than that of Demant or mine. He was concerned with throwing light on an historical problem from which he could distance himself and achieve without too much difficulty some perspective; Demant and I are trying to understand the society of which we are a part, which is changing as we analyse it, and from which we can only with great difficulty partially distance ourselves, in order to gain some perspective. The second reason why I have been bold and perhaps rash in this undertaking is that it is on a distinctly smaller scale than that of Tawney and Demant. The question immediately arose, Should I expand the Maurice Lectures? However I decided that having written them to a certain scale, there was no way of moderately expanding them (except for one theme which I mention below); they would have had to be greatly enlarged and become something very different. Apart from any other considerations, questions of time ruled that out in the immediate future. As it is I have concentrated on broad economic issues and the political and theological issues to which they give rise, and neglected other aspects of our society. This is even the case with industrial issues (except for passing references), although I have had a continuous concern for these as an amateur ever since I graduated.

Nevertheless I have expanded the Lectures at one point, in the first Dissertation. This term is of course used in universities for undergraduate or postgraduate work on a particular theme which is not on a sufficient scale to warrant the term 'thesis'. However I have taken the term from J. B. Lightfoot's classical nineteenth-century commentaries on Pauline epistles, Galatians (1865), Philippians (1868) and Colossians with Philemon (1875). Each of them included at the end extended essays on themes arising from the commentary, and several of these Dissertations – for example those on 'The Christian Ministry', 'St Paul and Seneca', and 'The Brethren of the Lord' – became classics in their own right. The first Dissertation in this book is an extended essay on Personal Freedom intended to fulfil the same function in relation to the Maurice Lectures as did those of Lightfoot to his Commentaries.

The second Dissertation reprints an evaluation of R. H. Tawney as a Christian Moralist, written in 1966. It is relevant here both because Tawney originally focused the twentieth-century discussion (it had been adumbrated long before Tawney or Weber), and because justice has not yet been done to his significance as a Christian thinker. I write with some feeling on this matter because I had the good fortune to be a pupil of R. H. Tawney when an undergraduate at the London School of Economics, where I gained a great affection and respect for him, and remained in occasional contact until his death. A research student of mine, Dr J. R. Atherton, Joint Director of the William Temple Foundation, Manchester, has just completed a doctoral thesis on Tawney as a Christian Social Moralist. At this point I must mention that Mr Atherton has made blunt and critical comments on the original drafts of the new material in this book, which have resulted in a greatly improved presentation. I have been much indebted to him even when I did not agree with him. Needless to say he bears no responsibility for defects that remain.

The other two essays were written near the time of the Maurice Lectures, one in 1975 and the other in the same year as they were (1977). They are reprinted because they deal with the same theme, that of Christian Ethics and current social change, and are not easily accessible. 'The Scene in Christian Social Ethics' is perhaps a little more popular in style and more disposed to wide generalizations. There are a number of other papers in Christian Social Ethics, not so immediately related to the theme of this book, which I hope to publish shortly. 'Reflections on Theologies of Social Change' originally appeared in *Theology and Change*, which I edited. It was intended as a *Festschrift* for the seventieth birthday of Alan Richardson, then Dean of York, but regrettably became a memorial volume.

It remains to thank the Dean of Salisbury, the Very Reverend Sydney Evans, who was in his last term as Dean of King's College, London, when the Maurice Lectures were delivered, for the kindness with which I was received and, together with him, Professor Gordon Dunstan, the first holder of the F. D. Maurice Chair in Moral and Social Theology at the College. My thanks are also due to my old friend and mentor Professor Arnold Nash, lately Professor of the Sociology of Religion in the University of North Carolina, for his comments; and not least to Mrs Brenda Peck, the Secretary in the Department of Social and Pastoral Theology in the University of Manchester, who has wrestled with an untidy and much altered manuscript, and to Miss Jean Cunningham of SCM Press.

The University of Manchester   Ronald H. Preston
All Saints' Day, 1978

I

The Maurice Lectures

— I —

Christian Critiques of Capitalism Reconsidered

It was a happy reparation to the memory of Frederick Denison Maurice when in 1933 W. R. Matthews, then Dean of the Faculty of Theology in King's College, London, instituted lectures to commemorate a man who was dismissed in 1853 from his two Chairs at the College, in English Literature and Modern History, and in Divinity, for denying the doctrine of eternal punishment. King's College has also honoured Maurice in a second and even more significant way, by the establishment in 1967 of the Chair of Moral and Social Theology called after him.[1]

The Maurice lecturer is not required to deal with Maurice himself, but I have searched for an appropriate theme and fixed on *Religion and the Persistence of Capitalism*. I have done this for two reasons. The first is that Maurice's name is inseparably linked with the recovery in this country of an explicit Christian social theology, especially within the Church of England, and above all with the experiment in thought and action, commonly known as Christian Socialism, in the period 1848 to 1854, even though it was only one of Maurice's many interests, and was more significant for the seeds it sowed than the thought or the experiment in Producers' Co-operatives it occasioned. The second reason is that in 1922 Professor R. H. Tawney, as he was later to become, delivered in King's College the first of the series of Scott Holland Lectures, subsequently published under the title *Religion and the Rise of Capitalism*. This book is a classic of English historical writing of this century, one to which I return again and again with renewed delight, both as to content and style. The theme was continued in a further series of Scott Holland Lectures given in 1949 at Oxford by Professor V. A. Demant[2] with the title *Religion and the Decline of Capitalism*. Now that another quarter of a century has gone by it seemed to me that the theme should be looked at again. Capitalism is tough. Perhaps the announcement of its decline was premature. Perhaps my title should have been 'Religion and the Transformation of Capitalism'. That will have to be considered.

In continuing this theme in a contemporary context I am certainly acting in the spirit of Maurice, who in the dedication to the Rev. Derwent Coleridge printed in the second and standard edition of his best known work, *The Kingdom of Christ* (1842), says 'No man I think will ever be of much use to his generation who does not apply himself mainly to the questions which are occupying those who belong to it.' There must, however, be a considerable difference in the scale of my treatment of the theme as compared with Tawney and Demant. In only three lectures I shall have to touch on many aspects of it which cannot be gone into thoroughly.

To begin with, a clarification of the terms of the discussion is needed. Tawney and Demant in using the term 'religion' meant the Christian religion in its personal and corporate aspects, and especially in its United Kingdom context. They did not discuss other religions, nor the position of Christianity in other continents such as Latin America. As to capitalism, it is particularly the institution of the free market and its implications which are the focus of attention; the place of wider sociological and cultural aspects of it, and how concentration on the free market has gone astray by ignoring them, follows from this. Also a discussion of capitalism inevitably brings in socialism as its ideal opposite, and the meaning of this term presents difficulties. Dr Angelo Rappoport in his *Dictionary of Socialism* (1924) listed thirty-nine definitions, and it is clear that the concept includes varied and sometimes contradictory elements. In this respect it is no different as a political and economic philosophy from the concepts of conservatism or liberalism, which equally do so. The element in socialism with which this discussion is particularly concerned is an emphasis on equality, for the sake of fellowship and community between persons, as distinct from a more individualistic way of looking at human beings.

Among the writers who have contributed to a Christian critique of capitalism in the last fifty years I shall concentrate on Tawney and Demant, with little or no explicit reference to other contributions from individual writers such as A. D. Lindsay, Josiah Stamp, William Temple, Denys Munby, John Sleeman, Charles Elliott, or corporate studies such as that of Ecumenical Conferences at Oxford in 1937 and Geneva in 1966, or recent Roman Catholic teaching.[3] Further, a new element has to be brought into the discussion, a query as to the persistence of religion itself. Religion in general is queried, particularly the Christian religion which has in fact had special attention. In a lively debate on secularization which has taken place in the last two decades or so in the Sociology of Religion, some have maintained that religion is inevitably on the way out in advanced economic societies. The case is far from proven, and I do not accept it, but in this discussion there will not be the space to give more than slight attention to it.

I

I start then with Tawney's *Religion and the Rise of Capitalism*. The question which preoccupied him was the change which came over the social theology of the church whereby a sense of the corporateness of human life was replaced by an individualist one, focused in its attitude to economic life. He points out that the medieval church started from the positions that (i) labour is necessary and honourable (ii) trade is necessary but perilous to the soul, and (iii) finance is at best sordid and at worst disreputable (p. 45). This last was expressed in the prohibition of usury, a term used in a narrow sense but also in a wider one to stand for any kind of extortion. Tawney traces the process of secularization both in political theory (pp. 19ff.; Machiavelli is specially mentioned), and in economic theory, which expressed itself in terms of mechanism instead of personal morality (pp.

45ff.). This led to the dissolution of a corporate view of society
as an organism whose members have different functions but
mutual and varying obligations. It was dissolved except for the
admittance of the necessity of what we might call 'ambulance
work' for particularly unfortunate cases. Human affairs came to
seem self-contained, and there was no longer an appeal to a
hierarchy of values of which the apex is religion. This led to
three consequences; first, instead of trying to become the basis
of a Christian civilization Christianity became acclimatized to a
secular one; second, it developed a sharp antithesis between
personal and business morality; and third, the church abandoned the endorsing of any particular social ethic or of any
attempt to enforce one as an obligation of church membership.

We should note that Tawney does not idealize the situation
whose break-up he studies. He exposes the gap between theory
and practice in the medieval world with irony and humour. Nor
does he think there should be no distinction between personal
and social morality. His criticism is that the church's traditional
social doctrines had nothing specific to offer in terms of the
growth of a capitalist economy, but were merely repeated when
they ought to have been thought out again from the beginning.
He says that they were abandoned because on the whole they
deserved to be abandoned. 'The social teaching of the Church
had ceased to count, because the Church itself had ceased to
think' (p. 188). The end result was a complacent acceptance of
acquisitiveness as an economic motive instead of a suspicion of
it. He concludes: 'Compromise is as impossible between the
Church of Christ and the idolatry of wealth, which is the practical religion of capitalist societies, as it was between the Church
and the State idolatry of the Roman Empire' (p. 280).

Let us look at Tawney's three points. The first one is that
Christianity, instead of trying to be the basis of a Christian
civilization, became privatized. Tawney has a typology of four
main outlooks with respect to the relation between Christianity
and social and economic institutions, each of which he says is to
be found in the church of the Middle Ages. They are, first, to
adopt an ascetic aloofness from these institutions; second, to

ignore them; third, to fight for utopian reforms; fourth, to accept them but criticize them (p. 30). It is interesting to compare these four types of outlook with the subsequent more refined typology of Richard Niebuhr in his classic *Christ and Culture*, which is itself a refinement of the typology in Troeltsch's monumental study, *The Social Teaching of the Christian Churches*. If we do this, it seems that Tawney's first position, to adopt an ascetic aloofness from social institutions and economic relations corresponds to Richard Niebuhr's 'Christ against Culture' type. Tawney's second position, to ignore these institutions, is a little obscure; but he probably means by 'ignoring' taking them for granted in a sense which implies no basic disagreement with them, and this would be an equivalent of Richard Niebuhr's 'Christ of Culture' type. Tawney's third and fourth positions, to fight for utopian reforms and to accept the institutions but criticize them, embody both Richard Niebuhr's 'Christ above Culture' and 'Christ the Transformer of Culture' types.

Richard Niebuhr's fifth type, 'Christ and Culture in Paradox', is not represented in Tawney. This is easy to understand, since it was not represented in the Middle Ages. It is particularly characteristic of Lutheranism with its doctrine of the Two Realms, or Two Kingdoms, that of God's right hand and his left. When Tawney comes to deal with Luther he does not bring out the value of a proper autonomy of economic thought and economic institutions from ecclesiastical control, which is the strong point of the Lutheran doctrine of the Two Realms and the ignoring of which has often led the Christian critique of capitalism astray, as we shall see. This proper autonomy is quite different from claiming that they should be totally autonomous, as Christian critiques of capitalism have often maintained that it does, and Tawney is inclined to do, though he is not quite consistent on the matter.

His failure to distinguish between Richard Niebuhr's two types, 'Christ the Transformer of Culture' and 'Christ above Culture', hides the main problem. He himself tends to write from a 'Christ above Culture' position, and perhaps this is why Professor D. G. MacRae can describe him as a 'mediaeval

schoolman'.[4] He was in fact much more than that, but the
position from which he wrote is one that has become increasingly impossible to hold, not only because the church ceased
to think, as he rightly said, but because the old form of church
control can no longer be maintained. Calvin's Geneva was an
attempt to maintain and indeed intensify it in the new situation
created by the Reformation, and Tawney did not like it. His
verdict is that Calvinism was at least consistent; it had little pity
for the poor but it did also try to make life unbearable for the
rich (p. 139). The problem is how to relate to economic institutions without trying to control them, as the 'Christ above Culture' position tried to do. Why could not that position be held?
Because of the process of secularization, intensified more recently by the growth of a plural society. In thought, secularization
has meant profound changes as a result of the scientific and
historical revolutions beginning in the middle of the seventeenth
century, so that, as Professor Owen Chadwick says at the conclusion of his masterly survey, *The Secularization of the European
Mind in the Nineteenth Century* (p. 265), the 'hallowed words' of
religion are now often understood in a radically different way.
In practice, secularization has meant a loss of control by the
church of institutions and activities. This has in fact also meant
a loss of influence, though a loss of control need not have that
effect. We now see that the link between Christian faith and
particular intellectual disciplines and institutions is more indirect. We cannot move directly to particular and fixed ethical
conclusions from either the Bible or Natural Law, which has
been the traditional way of reasoning. The church's traditional
teaching is now seen to be relative rather than fixed because of
our greater awareness of the cultural milieu in which it took
place, and the processes of cultural change which have happened since. Both the natural and social sciences have succeeded
in gaining a proper autonomy from ecclesiastical control. Questions are raised, especially about the social sciences, as to how
far they can be 'value free', but that they have developed tools
and delimited appropriate areas for study is clear; and whilst
their evidence must be sifted, we ignore it at our peril.

Tawney wrote of a Christendom position where church and state were 'one Jerusalem', to use a phrase of Archbishop Laud. He did not envisage a secular state. Many theologians (and sociologists like Talcott Parsons) have regarded this Christendom position itself as the secularization of the church because it became domesticated in a particular culture, and emancipation from it is seen as a liberation for the church and a purification of the Christian religion because it calls for active decisions on the part of adherents. Bonhoeffer is an example of a theologian who takes a similar position. He writes of the growth of autonomy, of the evolution of various areas of life towards self-responsibility. He did at one time use the term secularization, but he thought this sounded a condemnatory term so in the end he came to express the process to which he referred as that of 'the world coming of age' as against clericalization and hierarchical ecclesiastical structures. He writes of the Christian as being led by Christ crucified to a true worldliness and to living *etsi deus non daretur* (as if God were not given).[5]

If Christians are to see the sacred in the secular it involves a dialogue with the 'world', learning from it as well as teaching it. Religion cannot then be the cement of society in the way the state religion was intended to be in the Roman Empire, or as Christianity in the Christendom situation of the Middle Ages tried to be. This does not mean that Christians cease to believe that the church holds a concept of man which is distinctively its own, to quote Tawney again (pp. 278ff.). The question is how this view of man is to relate to economic and social institutions to-day.

Secularization is related to pluralism, and this has two aspects. One is that the Judaeo-classical-Christian outlook has so permeated the culture of Western societies that many who repudiate the Christian faith, even those who have turned secularization into an ideology of secularism, share much of its outlook. The other is a presence among us of believers in other ancient faiths. Pluralism could have the effect of producing a privatization of religion, to which Tawney refers which, whether it is embodied in much institutional expression or not, has little or no sense of social responsibility. But it need not. In Christian terms it could mean, first, the creation of a strong community among Christians themselves; second, a wider number of persons and groups connected with the church in various kinds of loose and informal ways; and third, a strong commitment to, and search for, the common good with those of other faiths and ideologies. This is not easy to achieve. It would be very different from the situation in the Middle Ages or at the rise of capitalism.

Tawney's second point refers to the development of a sharp antithesis between personal and social morality. He asks (p. 27): 'Can religion admit the existence of a sharp antithesis between personal morality and the practices which are permissible in business?' Clearly he expects the answer 'No, it can't'. He criticizes the teaching of the church in the sixteenth century as it grappled with the new economic forces for trying 'to moralize economic relations by treating every transaction as a case of personal conduct involving personal responsibility' (p. 187). The point is well taken in that it protests against a common failing, especially in Protestantism, to concentrate on the personal qualities of the Christian and ignore a theological evaluation of the social, economic, industrial and political structures within which the person operates; structures which both mould his outlook and circumscribe his range of behaviour.[6] Problems of corporate ethics and of those who act in a representative capacity are just as important as those of personal ethics. This century has seen a long struggle to recover them in Christian thought and it has some way yet to go. Whilst it would be too strong to talk of an antithesis between the two areas, there is a difficult relation between the two, hit off by the title, but still more the subject matter, of Reinhold Niebuhr's famous book, *Moral Man and Immoral Society*. One aspect of this is how to harness self-interest and at the same time control it for the common good. By self-interest I mean not just individual interest but its extension to the family. We shall be concerned with this later.

Tawney's third point concerns the abandonment by the church of the endorsing of any particular social ethic or of any

attempt to enforce one as an obligation of church membership.
In this matter Tawney was much influenced by Gore, to whom
Religion and the Rise of Capitalism is dedicated.[7] Gore reacted
against the Church of England establishment to such an extent
as to want to turn the church into a sect (to use Troeltsch's
typology). It is interesting that Gore wrote an introductory note
to the British edition of Troeltsch's *The Social Teaching of the
Christian Churches*, but he did not take its analysis to heart or he
would have seen the great difficulty, if not the sociological
impossibility (short of a revolution of the scale of that of 1917 in
Russia), of turning the church in this post-Christendom situation
into a sect, even if it were desirable. Theologically the Anglican
Church has never lived in a sectarian position and has no
theology of such a position. Institutionally it finds itself dealing
indeed with too much of an inappropriate Christendom structure, but with no possibility as far as one can foresee of abandoning it altogether. It has to take people in all the pluralist
confusion in which it finds them and deal with them on many
different levels. The idea of a sect with a specific ethic imposed
by church discipline seems out of the question, even if one could
be arrived at. In the Christendom situation, for instance, one
was clearly a marked person if excommunicated, a kind of social
pariah. Today no one would stay to be disciplined, nor would the
community at large notice if he were. He would just sever any
links with the church. Moreover since it is now no longer possible to make direct connections in the traditional way from the
Bible or church teaching to detailed ethical conclusions, there is
a range of options on most ethical issues, including economic
ones, likely to be open to the Christian. Empirical evidence and
its assessment will be involved in establishing these options, and
this implies the possibility of genuine differences of opinion between Christians on specific policies directed to achieving what
may be commonly accepted goals. Moreover sins no longer
stand out clearly as deviations from an agreed rule. It is in sex
ethics that by far the most effort has been made to inculcate one,
and in nearly every instance, perhaps all, it is now seen to
have been too narrow. But I must not be diverted into this area

of discussion. In other spheres efforts have been made unsuc-
cessfully to rule out for instance gambling, alcoholic drinks,
theatre going, and card playing from the Christian life. Again,
in economic ethics the teaching on usury broke down.

On the other hand a technique of raising moral questions in
the social and economic and other spheres can be developed
which sifts empirical evidence, discusses possible ways of acting
(sometimes conflicting ways), and asks leading questions of
advocates of all the ways to make sure they have faced the
problems raised by their own answers, and are sensitive to
questions raised by Christians disposed to take a different course.
It is a promising procedure, but it still leaves a wide range of
actions open. Questions of investments in South Africa have
recently been handled in this way, and so have violent and non-
violent methods of resistance to unjust regimes.

If the church were a tiny minority in an overwhelmingly
pagan situation it is possible that a definite code of behaviour
might be enforced as a matter of church discipline in the Christian community, but it seems quite unsuitable to our post-
Christendom situation, where we are faced by many levels of
believers and large numbers of post-Christian agnostics and
atheists. In this situation Christians will normally find themselves regarding those who remain within the law as not requiring church discipline.

A number of interesting questions emerge at this point. For
instance, how far is there a case for conscientious objection to
war or abortion, or more trivially to the fluoridation of the
water supplies, and how far should the state tolerate or over-
rule this objection? Then there is conduct which keeps within
the law but which is so shady as to warrant church discipline if
indulged in by a church member, supposing the member stays
to be disciplined. One thinks of Rachmanism in house-renting
as an instance. I cannot discuss these any further. For the present
I conclude that while particular groups within the church can
adopt specific ethical disciplines in issues which they are formed
to stress, for instance pacifism in one group, or the discipline
of living on the average income of wage-earners in another

group, the church itself is not able to establish the kind of discipline Tawney and Gore looked for. This does not mean that she should abandon responsibility for the economic realm, or be complacent about avarice and acquisitiveness. She has every reason to be alert to what is happening in the economic realm, to subject it to a theological critique and to be alert to the economic aspects of the church's own structures and operations. But church influence cannot be so direct as the Christendom situation presupposed, the situation whose break-up Tawney studied. It may well, however, be more profound. This point was made by A. D. Lindsay in a later series of Scott Holland Lectures, *Christianity and Economics*, which I must pass over.

II

V. A. Demant's *Religion and the Decline of Capitalism* takes up Tawney's first point about secularization and the autonomy of economic life and develops it further in a more broadly cultural direction. He is appreciative that all liberalism in its widest sense, as a force behind the development of economic individualism, has contributed to a creative personalism which is entirely congruous with a Christian understanding of man. But it has been at the cost of tremendous dislocation, and has unfortunately been tied to the theory of the free market and all that goes with it. It has raised up hostility against itself, disrupted the dispositions which reared and sustained it, broken up its own institutional framework, and been parasitic upon non-economic foundations of society. That is to say its autonomy got out of control and produced inhuman results because it had no integrating pattern of life behind it. That is why it is declining (p. 31). However to substitute state socialism is merely to echo collectively the individualistic fallacies of the capitalist past. A sense of citizenship is no substitute for occupational status; and the omnicompetent state is no better than the self-sufficient individual. A pluralism of power is necessary if personal freedom is to flourish (p. 154).

Demant's point that capitalism, in so far as it was assumed to work automatically, in fact depended upon an already existing non-economic substructure, is well made. What was taken for granted by advocating capitalism as 'nature' or 'natural', in the sense of not requiring human ordering, was in fact a complex net of non-contractual moral, legal and religious bonds which capitalism both assumed and at the same time undermined. Of course, talk of organic natural orders has often been understood in a static and over-conservative sense, and Demant is not free from this, but in principle he sees that a Christian understanding of Natural Law includes the fact that it is man's nature to share in God's freedom over his creation, so that a necessary dynamism is allowed for (p. 74).

There are three points from Demant which need attention. First, he is still talking within a Christendom framework. It is clear that what he calls 'the civic and agrarian society of the ancient and mediaeval worlds' (p. 83) is a kind of norm for him. So, as we shall see, he hardly ever does justice to the problem of production which capitalism has tackled pretty successfully. Further, that society is termed 'Christendom', and Demant clearly thinks its cultural values and economic and political achievements will not survive without a Christian basis. His position is very similar to that of T. S. Eliot in his *The Idea of a Christian Society* (1939). The greater understanding of secularization today, and the development of it since 1939, make it seem even more archaic now.[8]

Second, Demant has a very weak doctrine of the state. The reason for this is probably twofold. One is the experience, still recent when he delivered the lectures, of the totalitarian state in Nazism and Fascism, and the continuing Stalinist régime in the USSR. The other is that in the medieval world, which is something of a norm to him, the framework of the state was rudimentary. Now it is obvious there are great dangers associated with the state, not least a nation state, and Christians have tended to accept the authority of the *de facto* state too uncritically. But they have also tended to think of the state too negatively, as primarily a restrainer of disorder, underplaying its positive role in furthering the conditions for human flourishing. There are good theological as well as sociological grounds (into which I cannot go now) for regarding the state as a basic institution of society, as basic as the family. It is weak states, not strong ones, that we have to fear, always provided that part of the strength of a strong state includes checks on the misuse of its power. Demant quotes with approval (p. 104) a passage from F. A. von Hayek's *The Road to Serfdom* which stresses the danger of regarding the state as more than a piece of 'utilitarian machinery'. This phrase need not be given a minimizing interpretation; it could include the view of the state as a divine ordinance for human good, but Demant clearly allies himself with Hayek's minimizing view which can see no middle way between it and a collective state imposing moral views on all its citizens. This is surely a highly simplified polarization. Demant's fear of the omnicompetent state, valid enough against totalitarianism, seems misplaced when the problem now is whether in a self-conscious participatory 'Western' type of political democracy the electorate will be sufficiently far-sighted not to want incompatible things, and to allow the state enough power to guide the complex interlocked economies of advanced industrial societies in a way which avoids economic and social disasters. Demant is a high churchman with a low doctrine of the state.[9] This has been something of a twentieth-century Anglican weakness. Calvin knew better. He had a high doctrine of both church and state. And whatever excessive claims for itself papal teaching made for centuries over against the state, recent Roman Catholic teaching has had a more adequate doctrine of the state than that of Demant.

Third, Demant does not understand the working of the economic system. Perhaps that is why his announcement of the decline of capitalism is premature. After all, since he wrote, it has increased by 69% the Gross National Product of this country in the first twenty-five years of the Queen's reign.[10] Much of his pessimism is based on a false analysis of the working of the economic and monetary systems. This becomes clear in the last part of the book. It has been well dealt with by Denys Munby in the text and appendix of his book *Christianity and Economic*

Problems, and I do not intend to go over the ground again. Suffice it to say that if one is going to write of capitalism one does need to understand it. Demant has not been alone in this failure among Christian writers in this field. It led many in the 1930s to adopt uncritically the absurdities of the Social Credit monetary theory, propounded by the engineer Major Douglas and now almost entirely forgotten. (Demant himself advocated it at one time, though there is no explicit trace of this in the lectures that we are now discussing.) To do so was a particular characteristic of the former Christendom group.[11] A study of the effect of the ignorance of economics on the part of those who wrote so much about it on their whole diagnosis of modern society remains to be written and would be illuminating. Their faulty analysis led them to arrive by their route at the same conclusions as an over-simplified Marxist analysis, that capitalism is breaking down through its own contradictions.[12] The patient however is tougher than is supposed. Fortunately there have been accurate economic analyses by Munby, Sleeman and others, who have also given a theological critique of capitalism, a matter to which I shall return in the second lecture. For the present it is worth noting that underplaying the economic element in life in favour of the cultural one, as Demant is disposed to do, overlooks the fact that capitalism has removed the threat of starvation, which has been endemic in most of human history, from considerable areas of the globe. It has of course done a lot more. Its defenders would say that in doing so it has enlarged the area of human choice and thus of the moral life. There are few things more cramping than the threat of disease, famine and premature death.[13]

III

This whole discussion has presupposed the influence of Christianity in society, quite directly in the Christendom situation of the past and less directly today. Unless one starts with a rigidly Marxist position it seems sensible to suppose that religion can act as an independent variable, reacting reciprocally with economic and other factors. It is as impossible to prove this as it is impossible to prove the contrary of it. It is a question of the most reasonable presupposition. But even if it is granted, the influence is hard to measure or to state. The most famous hypothesis in this field, and one that lay behind Tawney's lectures, is that of Max Weber in *The Protestant Ethic and the Spirit of Capitalism*.[14] None has been so much discussed, so that it has become buried under the weight of the academic industry it has provoked. We now have even had a review of ' "The Max Weber Thesis" Thesis'![15] Weber assumed that some kind of correlation existed between Capitalism and Protestantism, for it had often been pointed out. What he did was to try to establish the details of the correlation, and after a study not only of the Christian religion but also for comparative purposes the religions of India and China, he found that it was an aspect of Calvinism which was particularly congenial to the capitalist spirit. According to this hypothesis disciplined acquisitive and ascetic behaviour was a means of making one's calling and election sure. In Weber's view religion is an independent source of insight which does not merely reflect the current situation but may well challenge it. Subsequently, however, those elements in the religious insight which are particularly relevant to believers in their particular situation are picked out and stressed by a process of what he called 'elective affinity'. This is what happened to Calvinism in the centuries after Calvin himself. The situation which proved so strong a factor in bringing to the fore this element in Calvinism was the spread of merchant, and later industrial, capitalism. New Testament scholars should not find strange this emphasis on the *Sitz im Leben* in the preservation of the tradition. It is how they think the message of Jesus was treated and preserved on its way to becoming embodied in the gospels. Weber in my judgment made his case.

Another example of the alleged influence of religion is that first articulated in depth by Élie Halévy in his *History of the English People in 1815*. He asks: What saved England from social revolution in the period 1790 to 1832? Why was England so stable in this period, compared with the upheavals in Europe?

He answers: The Wesleyan revival and its far-reaching effects on the religious and social life of England. Again this is difficult to prove, and again it is not a new point. It was thought at the time, for instance by Wilberforce, that a religious revival was the best safeguard against a threat to property and to political stability. The thesis may be hard to demonstrate with particular respect to Methodists as such, but it is plausible as far as the influence of evangelical religion as a whole is concerned, both in encouraging broad social conformity and in providing avenues for the fulfilment of social aspirations.[16]

What of the influence of religion today? How far is it influential in the persistence of capitalism? Even with the techniques of a sociologist of religion it is difficult to measure degrees of religiosity or religious commitment, that is to say the extent to which religious commitment influences actions and opinions in either personal or social terms, the more so because of the plural society in which we live. Therefore one hazards opinion with due caution. There certainly seems to be a bowdlerized version of a Protestant work ethic still with us, largely cut off from its religious roots. It is of questionable use at a time when in advanced industrial countries technological change, and especially the development of computerization, is rapidly increasing productivity. It is also taking more and more of not only the manual but also the mental drudgery out of life, and in doing so it is drastically reducing the scope for relatively unskilled production jobs, as it is increasing productivity per unit of input. One symptom of the remains of this work ethic is the readiness with which people talk of the jobless as scroungers when there are over one and a half million unemployed.[17]

Another factor is that in a time of diminished attendance the churches as institutions find themselves with the apparatus of a Christendom structure but without the means to support it. The effort to do so compels them to make the most of a property boom, or of gains from the rising value of development land,[18] and of the possibilities of the investment market generally. Of course other institutions such as universities and pension funds are in the same difficulty. But the position of the church is one of special poignancy, in view of the unjust structures in current capitalism, to find itself so entrenched in them. It is not that there is any way of avoiding this, unless the church were to adopt Bonhoeffer's plea that she should renounce all her endowments and live on the current offerings of the faithful, like the Taizé community in France. It would not be practical in the short term without great injustice to individuals to whom the church has commitments, and I doubt whether in the longer term it would be wise. It savours too much of a 'Christ against Culture' attitude; of the same type of mind that thinks the best way of avoiding the abuses of something like alcohol is to ban it altogether. But one would like to see more self-consciousness in the church of the likely effect of her economic interests on her outlook, in view of the pungent gospel reminder that one's heart is where one's treasure is. Does she not too readily accept the *status quo*? Lately pressures from within and without have begun to raise queries in various churches about investment policy, notably in relation to South Africa, and a greater self-consciousness is developing. It could go a good deal further. A realization that it is not possible for the church to live free from all questionable relations with economic systems is no reason for not keeping it and them under scrutiny.

If it be true that Christianity is now a sub-culture, as A. D. Gilbert (along with many others) maintains in his *Religion and Society in Industrial England: Church, Chapel and Social Change 1740–1914*, its direct influence on capitalism will not be as great either way as in the past, though it may still be of great significance for society. For instance no society can hold together politically or economically for any length of time without a considerable element of fellow-feeling and co-operation among its citizens. In so far as grandiose theories of *laissez-faire* ignored this they were foolish. Substantial sources of 'disinterested goodwill' are needed. The phrase is that of the sociologist Bryan Wilson. In his book, *Religion in Secular Society* (1966), negative as it was about religion, he ended by seeing religious sects as a prime source of this necessary element. Ten years later, in *Contemporary Transformations of Religion*, he is even more pessimistic about the future of religion

and, logically enough therefore, pessimistic about the future of
Western society. There is much to dispute in his analysis in both
books, but any Christian believer, whether a member of a sect
or church, can hardly fail to see disinterested goodwill as an
expected fruit of his faith. The problem is how to harness this to
a creative response in the society in which he lives, and not let it
dissipate in ineffective and sentimental because irrelevant
actions.

The church is called by reformers to be prophetic. On the
other hand sociologists frequently point to the sustaining and
conserving role it plays. Guenter Lewy's study of *Religion and
Revolution* maintains that critics of organized religion have often
exaggerated its integrating role and minimized its revolutionary potential. He thinks this is partly because revolutionary
periods in human history have been less than periods of political
tranquillity. Whether this is so or not we are hardly in a period
of political tranquillity now. Lewy's case studies are designed to
show the Janus-face of religion, not least in that it can often
work both in an integrative and revolutionary way at the same
time. He himself realizes that a convincing verification of his
conclusion involves formidable and perhaps insoluble problems.
But in these matters complete verification eludes us; the most
we can hope for is the demonstration of plausible correlations of
the kind established by Max Weber. In this sense Lewy's con-
tention does seem plausible. It is perhaps fruitless to speculate
how far the church in this country can preserve the substance of
the Christendom structure. The danger of the attempt to do so
is such a growing preoccupation with the effort to keep its present structures going as to drive out a proper social concern. In
effect this is a profoundly conservative stance. Yet we cannot
say this is inevitable. The polar opposite would be more like that
pictured by Karl Rahner in *The Shape of the Church to Come*, a
church built from below by 'basic communities', being constantly renewed by free decisions of faith, and with congrega-
tions being formed within a secular society bearing no imprint of
Christianity. This could indeed happen, but it would be rash to
say it is inevitable. The reality is likely to be less clear cut. In

any event the problem of relating the integrating and the dynamic elements in the Christian faith, the prop and the spur, remains.

I shall turn to problems of relating these two roles in the third lecture. But before that it is necessary to look more closely at the economic problems which any society has to solve, with special reference to the way capitalism tries to solve them and whether socialism solves them any better. On this basis we may see more clearly where traditional Christian critiques have been inadequate, in the hope of providing a more adequate one.

— 2 —

Ambiguities in Capitalism and Socialism Today

When a moral theologian lectures on a theme like 'Ambiguities in Capitalism and Socialism Today', the question is bound to arise, What is the status of his remarks? He obviously cannot derive them solely from Biblical Studies, or Church History, or Systematic Theology, or any of the classical theological disciplines. His theological studies provide him with a basic stance or orientation by which he interprets the heights and depths of human life. Indeed everyone has a basic orientation, explicit or implicit, through which he interprets the basic 'facts' of life. Mine is the Judaeo-Christian one. However, in examining contemporary economic systems he needs also not only the competence which ought to be possessed by anyone who seeks to be well informed on public affairs, he must also draw upon a certain expertise in the social sciences which he may not personally possess. How then can he escape the charge of amateurishness and presumption?

These questions indicate a genuine dilemma. Once it is clear that we cannot proceed directly from the Christian tradition, whether the Bible or Natural Law or Systematic Theology, to conclusions in the spheres of various specialist studies, in this case economics, industry and politics, there is no escape from coming to grips with the empirical data in those fields and mastering the various intellectual disciplines needed to cope with them, the moral theologian cannot do so on the basis of his discipline alone. Ideally this is a co-operative enterprise, an interdisciplinary one. More and more this activity is seen to be necessary.[1] Sometimes when group activity is not immediately possible he can produce the material by himself, but in fact drawing upon the experience of other individuals and groups, together with any special competence he may happen to possess. In this case I am following the latter process.[2] The analysis that I am about to make draws upon a mixture of theological resources and empirical studies. It is a personal assessment which draws on the work of many others and many group studies. Moral theologians do not lay down a law from above, they try to clarify issues from within, in association with those of relevant experience of them, whether experts or lay folk. Therefore my diagnosis, whilst it asks for serious attention, also asks that those who disagree with it should advance other reasoned considerations where they consider mine erroneous or incomplete.

There is an inescapably hazardous element in all such enterprises. However well buttressed interdisciplinary work may be, however well the necessary expertise is drawn upon, we find in every discipline that within the broad lines of the subject there are different schools of thought, and that the experts differ. It is often said that where you find three economists there will be four opinions. It was partly because of this that the Christians we were considering in the last lecture thought they were entitled to ignore the subject altogether and invent their own, or adopt the thought of 'cranks', not realizing that there is a core of the subject which underlies the different schools of thought and to which a proper autonomy has to be allowed. The matter is yet more difficult in that now and again those whom the established authorities have considered cranks have later been proved right after all.[3] There is no escape from careful discrimination, and no guarantee that a moral theologian by himself, or a group with which he works and on which he draws, may not make errors of diagnosis. We can be alert to the dangers, and devise methods of trying to reduce them (and here the study of issues of Christian social ethics in the Ecumenical Movement has pointed the way), but it is impossible to be sure that they have been overcome. In any case there remain irremovable uncertainties about present trends and future situations in studying social processes of which one is a part as one studies, and which do not stay still whilst one is studying them. That is why there are no simple 'Christian' solutions to ethical problems, but a general Christian orientation to them and, after empirical investigations, a range of considerations and options to be borne in mind (though there may well be certain courses of action which practically speaking can be ruled out).

In interdisciplinary work the moral theologian has his own part to play. One is to be alert to open or unavowed doctrinal and moral presuppositions in what appears to be, as presented, 'scientific' in the sense of value-free. There has been a tendency for theologians to move from ignoring the proper autonomy of other disciplines to becoming uncritical of them. This has sometimes happened in the field of pastoral counselling with respect to various schools of psychology, and it is characteristic of the Liberation Theologians of Latin America with respect to Marxism. But to pursue these themes would take me too far afield, and after these preliminary cautions I turn to the specific theme of this lecture.

I

I begin with the basic economic problem which every society has to solve and which is the subject matter of economics, that is how to allocate scarce resources which can enter into the economic system and which have alternative uses. There are far more things that human beings would like to do with the resources that are available to them than they are able to do, and a selection must be made. To an economist the real cost of something is the alternatives which might have been undertaken if those which have in fact been chosen had not been chosen. It is a study of this problem which makes economics autonomous, to use the term frequently used in a pejorative sense by R. H. Tawney and others.[4] Some economists are more ambitious and try to apply economic analysis to every aspect of life. Professor Gary Becker, for instance, in *The Economic Approach to Human Behaviour* applies economic techniques to the question of mar-

riage, and decides that marriage will occur if the expected benefits exceed the costs in the sense of opportunities foregone. I leave
this hazardous enterprise aside as hardly relevant to our concerns, and return to the basic economic problem of any society,
the need to maximize scarce resources.

Within this problem are subsidiary problems, such as how to
register demands for goods and services, how to see that the
production of them matches the demand for them, how to
decide the distribution of rewards for producing them, and how
to allocate resources between present consumption and future
consumption. The only strictly economic value is the avoidance
of waste. If resources are scarce it seems to the economist a pity
to waste them by using them less efficiently than they might be
used. But an economist will always add that this consideration
is 'other things being equal'. He must admit that it is only one
value among others, and that there may be many reasons why
one would not wish to maximize resources in particular instances. Nevertheless the economist thinks it is as well to be aware
of the cost of alternatives foregone if one does not maximize
them, and not cover up the cost by camouflage. To take an
example, the National Coal Board has since the war reduced the
mining force from three quarters of one million to one quarter
without undue social hardship. We have all paid more for our
coal in order that this should happen than otherwise we would
have done, but most people would agree that it was an economic waste well spent.

The two classical economic systems to solve society's basic
economic problems are that of the free or market economy and
that of the demand or planned economy. The first is commonly
called capitalism, the second socialism. I am treating them as
ideal types.[5] Let us consider capitalism first. The theory of the
free market presupposes minimal state activity. What are
economically 'correct' results occur automatically as a by-
product of individuals rationally pursuing their individual interests. By doing so they ensure that either profits or losses are
made, through the process of competition; in the end the things
that are wanted are made because those who make them make

profits, and those that are not wanted are not made because those who make them make losses. That is the freedom of consumer choice. The consumer is king. He exercises liberty and creativity; and this is necessary to man as a moral being.

Adam Smith is often regarded as the theorist of the free market, both in his *The Wealth of Nations* (1776) and in his *The Theory of Moral Sentiments* (1759), which underlies his later book. Adam Smith's problem was, How can individuals be led to behave in ways which will serve the common good? The answer he gave is, By making use of their self-regarding motives in an environment of freedom, so that men are led by an invisible hand to promote an end which was not part of their intention. The search for personal satisfaction and material wealth is a 'beneficent deception imposed by nature'. Adam Smith was well aware of what he calls 'the clamorous importunity of vested interest', especially of the rich and the business corporations, which need extensive state activity to restrain them, even though he had a strong sense of the sheer incompetence of the state. He also saw a prominent role for the state in education, because of the deleterious effects of specialization through the division of labour,[6] and he thought that the prosperity of the working people was a true measure of a country's advance. He regarded the free market as the least bad way of organizing the economy because economic motives, though far from the best, are the most reliable and persistent ones. By this means even the most selfish person is compelled to work for the common good through the automatic working of the free market.

Subsequent apologists of the free market system have not got much further than Adam Smith, though they have dotted the i's and crossed the t's of what he said. Let us take two examples. The first is Professor F. A. von Hayek, the economist, whose book *The Road to Serfdom* was widely read when it appeared in 1944.[7] He has pursued the theme of the political philosophy needed to underpin economic individualism in a series of books since then. Two of the latest are under the general title of *Law, Legislation and Liberty*; the first is *Rules and Order* (1973) and the second, *The Mirage of Social Justice* (1976). Hayek's position is that as soon as men get beyond tribalism they have to find some method of living together without sharing common ends; just because man is indeterminate society will not be in agreement about specific ends. Therefore we need to arrive at a rule of abstract justice, so that men who are no longer dominated by the group can follow their own individual devices, whether these are co-operative or not, and hence can have the chance of exercising their creativity. We need an impersonal mechanism to integrate individual actions, and the coercive powers of government should be restricted to a minimum in favour of spontaneous order. This is the justification of the free market and competition. He is not willing to trust the citizen as a voter in the way in which he is as a consumer, because the issues of political decision are dangerously remote from the voter, whereas his economic decisions in the market are immediately present to him, and because each of us is irremediably ignorant of many factors on which the attainment of our ends depends. Indeed he stresses the unforeseen consequences of decisions, and our proneness to assume knowledge which we do not possess. For this reason he is unwilling to let human planning do more than a minimum in directly determining the nature and shape of institutions.

The cost of the free market is borne by those who are inefficient or obsolete. They will ask for social justice, and this will require them to be propped up by those who are more efficient and not obsolete. This will in turn seriously diminish economic progress. Socialism is a return to tribalism (though Hayek is willing to allow that a minimum wage is necessary). Hayek's ideal is an individualism which will lead to the growth of knowledge and what he would call material and cultural progress. He is critical of the conservative for being too fearful of change, too deferential to established authorities, and too nationalistic. His defect is so to ignore the deep roots of the organic and corporate side of human life (which of course has its own dangers), as to produce a theory of economic society which human beings will simply not accept in anything like the pure form in which it is presented.

A similar position is taken by the Chicago economist Professor Milton Friedman, in his book, *Capitalism and Freedom*. Taking the freedom of the individual, or perhaps the family, as a basic requirement Friedman argues that they should make their own choices about what they want, and then pay for it directly themselves. This would include things like schools and highways. The only exceptions to this would be when it is impossible to tell the extent to which any particular person benefits directly from what he calls the 'neighbourhood effect'; in this case the community as such would be charged. Competitive markets transform the self-interested actions of individuals into social benefits. Policy making is too difficult to be left to policy makers, it is far better left to some automatic device like the free market. It is this position which has led Friedman so strongly to emphasize monetary measures as the sole way of dealing with inflation. He has faith in the automatic working of monetary policies, and will not entertain wage or price controls as alternatives or complements to anti-inflationary monetary restrictions. He is, however, prepared to advocate one striking modification of the free market. He is the inventor of the scheme for a negative income tax which would guarantee an unconditional basic minimum income for all, in order to cope with those who are the victim of circumstance. But it would be a very minimum income.

Similar theories of the free market to those of Hayek and Friedman were accepted by many Christians in the nineteenth century, perhaps most Christian leaders for a large part of the century. It was not because they wanted to dissociate economic life from morality and leave it autonomous, a charge that has often been laid against them, but that they saw the free market on the one hand as an attack on unjustified privilege, and on the other they thought that laws on social and economic questions should be as free of moral compulsion as possible. It was not the duty of the state to impose morality in matters best left to the individual. They carried this further into making a distinction between poverty and indigence. True, they often appeared to condemn the poor as such, but the more perceptive did not go so far. Poverty, they held, was necessary in a well constituted society, and honourable; whilst indigence was due to lack of foresight and to extravagance and was a punishment of God (except in the case of something that could not have been safeguarded against, such as the onslaught of blindness). This led them to make a basic distinction between the deserving and undeserving poor, a distinction that we have been trying to move away from ever since the minority report of the Poor Law Commission (1909), written by the Webbs.

The Christians who took this view of the free market system ignored a number of considerations which have become much clearer since their time. One is the moral framework which capitalism presupposes and to which they paid little attention, as Demant pointed out. Also they often overlooked the considerable state framework necessary to prevent the abuses of the free market. Further, they were complacent about the great inequalities of income which the free market developed, aided by the system of inheritance, which made those who were well off able to command the resources in the market for luxuries which those who were poor could not command for necessities. With inequalities of wealth, of course, also went inequalities of power. They did not see that the beauties of the automatic mechanism which they admired so much seemed like blind fate to vast numbers of ordinary people who less and less were willing to put up with it. And although they would have denied the fact, they gave little attention to the many other aspects of man's life than the economic, such as the desire to love, the desire to play, the desire to exercise power over others, all of which need to be given attention in any economic social and political system. Moreover they underemphasized the ingenuity shown by the managerial side in subverting the free market to obtain special advantages for itself.[8] It is also interesting in this connection to contrast the comparative secrecy in which management and directors can operate in industry with the greater publicity which governs all trade union activities.

Full allowance must be made for the enormous achievements of capitalism, not least through the mobilization of capital by limited liability and the incentives for the entrepreneur to take

risks which this created. It has sustained an unprecedented increase in population and at the same time in the standards of
life in those parts of the world where it first developed. A lot of
social aims have been achieved which seemed hopeless in the
nineteenth century. Behind these triumphs of industrialism and
making it possible were the previous revolutionary changes in
the traditional patterns of agriculture. Together they have produced a social transformation.[9] In particular the opening up of
the North American plains to grain production produced much
better working-class diets and health in the Western world, and
therefore much more working-class energy. Energy went into
self-help, and self-help led to adult suffrage. The Malthusian
bogey was well and truly laid.

However other factors than that of the free market were of
importance even at the heyday of that market. One was sanitary
reforms, especially that of the water supply. It was the necessity
of combating epidemics like cholera which was the first solvent
of *laissez-faire* theory, if only because it was no respecter of
persons and spread to the rich as well as the poor.[10]

The problem now is to bring forward the economic development of the Third/Fourth World. This clumsy designation
seems necessary to distinguish the oil-rich states from the rest,
from whom the crippling burden of poverty must be removed as
it has been from us. We need to go beyond the 'green revolution'
(which in some ways has been a disappointment), not only by
building up food reserves, but by the kind of investment in
Fourth World farming which builds up self-help and dignity
and provides the basis for a growth in manufacture. These are
major questions, to which I refer again briefly in the third
lecture, but which for the most part must be left aside.

If capitalism was not able to triumph on its own terms even
in its heyday, further questions arise today. In our world, the
industrial West, growth has continued steadily until recently,
when we had a temporary check with a 6% fall in the standard
of living, which has since been recovered. It has however continued at a cost. There has been a sequence of booms and slumps
with their periodical bouts of cyclical unemployment, and now

a threat of structural unemployment, as I mentioned in the last lecture (p. 18). Further, the free market is becoming less and less a consumer's market, and more and more dominated by very large producers.[11] I refer of course to the multi-national companies. It is not easy to find the facts about them because they keep their operations shrouded in mystery for tax accountancy reasons. But leaving multi-nationals in particular aside, and turning to the general question of large firms, it is worth noting that although there are half a million companies in Britain, one per cent of them accounts for half our industrial assets, output and trade. The last major industrial census showed that in twenty of the twenty-two main sectors of industry and services an average of four or five firms accounted for half the assets; banking and insurance was the chief exception.[12] Again a hundred top companies in this country produced 20% of our manufacturing output in 1950, 50% in 1970, and that percentage is still growing. Export trade is even more concentrated. Thirty-one companies account for two-fifths of our exports. Much the same position is found if other countries in the EEC are examined, or indeed the USA. Size is also decisive when it comes to investment, in the shape of internally generated funds, for apart from these the major source of savings is insurance and pension funds, and these have recently been more interested in land and government securities than industry.

Then there are inequalities of wealth and income and therefore of power. We have a Royal Commission enquiring into the distribution of income and wealth, and certain interesting data have already emerged from reports which it has issued. For instance, as far as income is concerned, in the year 1972/3 the top half of the country received three-quarters of the pre-tax incomes and the bottom half received one-quarter. Also at the moment tax policy is working counter to social policy because of (i) the erosion of the value of personal and child tax allowance in a period of inflation, (ii) the elimination of the reduced rates of income tax on lower earnings. Or to turn to the ownership of capital assets, in 1973 the top 1% owned 27·6% of the personal wealth of the country, the top 5% owned 51·3% of it. The percentage of wealth owned by the 1%, by the very rich, has fallen, but the beneficiaries have been those next nearest down the scale. If we take earned incomes, a top executive gets fifty times more pay before tax than an agricultural worker. It is extremely hard to see how such a differential can be justified. This relationship has hardly changed since 1913. The report produced in 1977 by the National Institute of Economic and Social Research, *Poverty and Progress in Britain, 1953–73*, shows that the relation of low incomes to medium incomes is the same as in 1953.[13] That is to say, the poor have shared in the economic expansion since then, but there has been no significant redistribution of wealth within the country. In general it remains true that the most interesting and the least dangerous jobs are the best paid. Even within much more closely economically related sectors of the working population very considerable divisions and differences exist. The difference between the blue-collar and the white-collar worker extends very far. In questions of sick pay, hours of work, holidays, length of notice, eating facilities and the extent of absence allowed for domestic emergencies, the white-collar worker is much better off than the blue-collar. And within the ranks of the blue-collar worker the financial disadvantage of the low-paid is not compensated by greater access to the social services but the reverse; a cycle of deprivation is set up which begins with infancy and has already sown lasting fruits before pre-school days are over. I have mentioned these problems produced by capitalism. Are they frictions, which in principle can be overcome, or are they endemic? Do they indeed indicate that capitalism is unworkable?

There have been various theories suggesting that there are inherent contradictions in capitalism which will cause it to collapse. The Marxist challenge is the most famous, but it is much less confident now than it used to be. According to the classical Marxist theory there should be under capitalism a growing impoverishment of the worker, a fetter upon production, a very clear distinction between productive and unproductive labour, and a surplus value which is taken by the employer from what by rights should go to the worker, and this in turn leads to chronic underconsumption and a crisis in the capitalist system. None of this seems plausible today. A discussion of the now various forms of Marxism is not possible on this occasion. I am concerned only to indicate that its economic theories, possibly its weakest element in any case, are remote from our present situation.

However, we have recently had a new theory about the collapse of the economic system, that put out by the Club of Rome in its well known report, *The Limits to Growth* (1972). Allied with this is *The Ecologist*'s report, *A Blueprint for Survival* (also 1972 and revised in 1977), concerned with the dangers to human life by the fouling of the atmosphere and the dislocation of the ecosystem as an added result of the rapacious development of modern economic society. It is true that the attack goes beyond capitalism, in the sense that it covers a demand economy as well, but this is a convenient moment to refer to it. The Club of Rome report worked with a series of factors, population size, food production, industrial production, the amount of pollution, and the rate of use of non-renewable resources. It came to the conclusion that, assuming these grow at the present rate exponentially (that is steadily over the years at a constant annual per cent), within a hundred years global society will reach an impasse. At the same time the ecologists pointed out that we are in danger of exceeding the absorptive capacity of the biosphere; that is, we are producing a level of pollution of earth, air and water which will no longer be self-correcting.

The ecologists have certainly issued an important warning which is a check to the over-confidence which has characterized some of the technical and economic developments since the war, when our rate of monitoring has not kept pace with our rate of technical change. Once this is pointed out, however, it is not in principle difficult to correct, nor exceptionally expensive in economic resources. There is no reason to suppose that the danger cannot be coped with, even though one must not automatically assume that it will be coped with. As to the *Limits to Growth* report, though widely acclaimed by the public, it has received a great deal of serious technical criticism. It has been modified to some extent by subsequent work done by the Club of Rome, which has now issued its fourth Report, but it was the first report which made the impact by its sensational conclusions.[14] What is basically overlooked is an exponential increase in technical innovation which is matching the other exponential increases it mentioned. Suffice it to say that neither the Club of Rome nor the ecologists have shown that the free market system, or indeed any of the advanced economic systems of the world, is likely to collapse.

A more cogent analysis of a contradiction in capitalism is provided by Professor Fred Hirsch[15] in *The Social Limits to Growth* (1977). He points out that the paradox of the relative affluence that we have achieved is that it is unsatisfying when widely spread, once the basic necessities of food, clothing, and shelter are secured. Perhaps we might go further and add to them our modern entertainment devices like television, or labour-saving devices like washing machines. Beyond these, and it is not certain what percentage of the economic productivity of the economy this amounts to, there arise what he calls 'positional goods' which are either absolutely scarce or socially scarce. He refers, for instance, to the enjoyment of scenery, the pleasure of suburban living, and access to leadership positions. In these 'positional goods' the problem arises that, to use his favourite phrase, 'if everyone stands on tiptoe no one sees better'. The positional good depends on relative scarcity; the more people possess it, the greater the pressure of time needed to amass enough to possess it and then to consume it. Also this increase on the one hand leads to less sociability between people and, on the other, acts as a stimulus to wage inflation. To see economic advance, or rather social economic advance, as individual advance writ large is to set up expectations that can never be fulfilled. Adam Smith's invisible hand only worked in the earlier stages of capitalism.

Hirsch reinforces the point made by Demant, that capitalism always required social foundations which were laid in a different kind of society. It required what we might call the old-fashioned virtues. That is to say its reliance on self-interest actually implied a commitment to truth, to honesty, to trust, to respect for law, and to a sense of social obligation to prevent theft, fraud and breach of contract, and to ensure the uprightness of legislators and judges. These were not derived from, nor cultivated by, capitalism itself but came from three other sources; traditional social ties in the community, religious teaching and a sense of civic duty. One of Hirsch's worries is that it is only this last which may be left. Capitalism not only did not foster these virtues, it eroded them. This has been the effect of the greater anonymity and mobility produced by advanced industrial capitalism. The rationalist individualist knows that he does best when everyone else co-operates socially and he does not. It is therefore vitally important for people to behave at least *as if* they were altruistic, and to put social interests much higher in their priorities. In short, a strong supporting social morality is needed if the economic system is to work. Universal suffrage with the consequent rising expectations makes more demands on an attenuated moral base. There is also needed much more collective provision of the positional goods so that they are partly removed from the commercial sector of the economy, in the hope that more space will be created for the non-economic aspects of life. Hirsch has made a powerful case, not I think so much for the social limits to growth as for the social limits to private consumption. This requires very careful attention, though it does not show, nor does he say that it shows, that the free market capitalist system of itself is necessarily collapsing, though it requires considerable amendment.

The likely scenario is still economic growth. Indeed it is possible that the vastly greater productivity from technical resources, which is more and more characteristic of our time, may enable us to make a serious inroad into the appalling poverty which still cripples so many parts of the world. The danger is that we shall not do this, but use our wealth to live in a wealthy ghetto in a global slum. But whether we do or not, I do not think that any of the theories of the inevitable collapse of the market economy have made their case.

II

I turn now briefly to look at the command economy, commonly called socialism. This involves the state planning of the allocation of scarce resources, including the allocation of labour, and of funds for investment as against current consumption. The achievement of the command economy in industrially backward countries has been very great. There has been an enormous process of rapid industrialization, made possible by a policy of forced savings. This chiefly involves the absence of the production of consumer goods. In effect a rate of saving is imposed on the population by the political authorities who are irremovable at the polls; this would be inconceivable if they were removable. Also command economies have no unemployment; they simply do not allow people to be unemployed. Moreover there is little inflation. Also the peasant has been freed from the control of the local landowner and money-lender who have oppressed him from time immemorial; and with the abolition of inheritance, inequalities of wealth cease to be a problem, though inequalities of income may still be great. In China, however, they are reputed to be no greater than in the ratio of eight to one.[16]

The economic vision of command economies has been economic growth with stability, just like the economic vision of the free market economies. It is for this reason that in recent years there has been a revolt against both by some radically-minded members of the younger generation, usually from the more affluent parts of the world, who do not see the point of an indefinite pursuit of further affluence. However, they usually presuppose the level of affluence these societies have already attained. It is not clear how far they will maintain this attitude in a less favourable economic climate than a decade ago, but it is important that it is not altogether lost.

The difficulties of the command economies have been also noteworthy.[17] The efficient planning of so many economic decisions is a virtual impossibility, beyond the competence of mortal man (that is of course why the beauties of doing a lot of it automatically in the free market have their attraction). It has been impossible for the central authorities to make all the decisions governing input and output, and a great deal of blockage and waste results. (Our forms of the market economy have of course their own waste.) However it is possible that the development of computers will facilitate the co-ordination of vast numbers of factors in a way not possible before, and therefore make easier the self-management of industrial units without recourse to the market system, though it is hard to see it ever working in this respect with the same facility as the free market. Nevertheless there seems to be no fundamental reason, though there are many political difficulties in the way, why the command economy of the Soviet Union should not work towards a system in which the basic over-all decisions are taken centrally, leaving the rest of the economy to react from the pressures of the market resulting from the central economic (including fiscal) policies. This is similar to the way the market economies are developing.

The costs of the command economy however are mainly political ones. They are the concentration of political and economic power in the same source, and the development of a bureaucracy run by a new power élite in which the white-collared intelligentsia predominate. Trotskyites and some other groups of the Left have held that this was due to some peculiar faults of Stalin, or perhaps of some group of which he could be said to be a part, but this is very implausible. In order to understand it one needs to use the techniques of a sociological analysis of élites and of stratification processes of society in a command economy precisely similar to that which one can apply in a 'Western' market economy. Yugoslavia is the command economy which has made the clearest effort to escape from these problems. Yet even here management has got into the hands of paid professionals, and it is clear that collective bargaining is still needed. Moreover if there is to be effective collective bargaining it is necessary for the workers to have their own independent sources of information, and this has profound political implications. What seems clear is that under socialism conflicts

of interest remain between, for instance, the givers of orders and
the receivers of them. Differentials also remain; and so do
different levels of access to privileges. The end of private ownership does not bring an end to all these, nor to the end of political
and economic despotism. Nor does the state begin to wither
away, as in the pure Marxist theory it should. Nor does nationalism cease to be a powerful force, which also in Marxist theory it
should. Indeed there are signs that the reverse is the case. And if
one moves to consider the general quality of life there seems
little doubt that problems of, for instance, suicide, drug addic-
tion and mental illness, are as bad in the advanced command
economies as in the free market economies. But if one asks, Are
they collapsing? the answer must be 'No'. It is true that the
need for entrepreneurial and managerial skills (which Lenin
thought nothing of since he assumed that anybody who could
add up was capable of exercising them) in order to reduce block-
ages and to satisfy speedily rising consumer expectations,
seems likely to lead to more use of free market techniques co-
existing within the over-all command economy. If it does so it will
probably be a gradual and not a dramatic process; and there is
no reason to suppose that any factor is leading to the necessary
collapse of these economies. In fact there is no evolutionary
tendency at work to produce either the collapse of capitalism or
the advent or collapse of socialism.[18] These grandiose theories of
the progress of history are all discredited. This perhaps illustrates
the folly of the kind of Trotskyite or anarchist of the Left who
thinks that if he secures the collapse of the present system
socialism will emerge as a result of the collapse. All the evidence
suggests that whenever anything like this technique has been
applied its results have led not towards socialism but towards a
revolution of the Right.

III

However we do not live under either a simple free economy or a
simple command economy. In the West we veer between a
social democracy where the emphasis is rather more on the
political process of participatory democracy, and democratic

socialism where the emphasis is rather more on the public control of economic activities. The situation is changing all the
time. For instance the state is taking over in many countries not
just basic monopolies but companies operating against others in
the market economy as well. In this country, for instance, there
are British Leyland and BP and the activity of the state in companies like Rolls Royce and Chrysler. Are these half-way houses,
if we may so call them, workable? They are certainly limited by
the extent to which a purely national economy has limits set
upon it by international economic factors; even the strongest
economy, that of the United States, is not free from external
constraints.[19] But whether the mixed economies are workable is
more a political than an economic problem.

The problem is that of reconciling group conflicts and group
expectations. Certainly the efficiency which the economist
wishes for is necessary to avoid waste but, to quote the words
of Tawney, 'To convert efficiency from an instrument into a
primary object is to destroy efficiency itself.'[20] The reason is
that if you destroy co-operation you insult self-respect. The
problem is that we all gain by creativity, and creativity means
change, and we also all have a vested interest in job security and
stability, which militates against change. The problem of a
participatory democracy as far as economics is concerned is that
the government is bound to have more responsibility, because
of the inadequacies of a purely automatic system, for reasons
that we have already discussed, but now it also has to secure the
broad agreement of the entire population, not least the organized body of workers who, until recently, could very largely be
ignored. This requires an informed political and industrial electorate which can see beyond the end of its political and economic nose. It requires a sense of the common good and a sense
of fairness. It requires the qualities of prudence and proportion
which are traditionally emphasized in Christian ethics. And it
requires governments who lead, who are prepared to implement
unpopular policies where necessary, and at the same time are
sensitive to those who have less power in either industrial or
political weighting.

The easiest line for them is to by-pass the problems of injustice by economic growth, but when international factors do
not permit the buying off of competing claims, the next easiest
policy is to resort to inflation, which makes matters worse. The
lucky and the unscrupulous in the use of power are the ones who
benefit at a time of inflation. Yet governments cannot easily
deflate because of the danger of creating an unacceptable level
of unemployment. At the moment we are doing this at the expense very largely of teenagers who are less powerful politically
than other sections of the community. We all want stable prices
and full employment and most of us want free collective bargaining. The three are incompatible. How to achieve the right
mix between the three calls for the highest art of government.
There is no reason to suppose, however, that it is inherently
impossible to achieve, and therefore no reason to suppose that
either social democracy or democratic socialism is necessarily
unworkable. In particular there is no inherent reason why elements of a command economy in the shape of planning cannot
be mixed with elements of a market economy to make the
market a better instrument for maximizing public benefit.
Doubtless it will be rough and ready, like all political and
economic processes. The main problem is to secure consistent
policies rather than patchy ones. This requires political wisdom
from both government and electorate, and this in turn requires
moral wisdom. But this is what politics is about.[21] What is clear
is that both types of social democracy present very considerable
challenges to the maturity of their constituencies.

However there is the further problem. An individualistic and
hedonist outlook is not a sufficient basis for any society. This
was ignored by classical capitalism, and its *laissez-faire* view is its
most serious and fundamental defect. Classical socialism realized
this, but overlooked inherent conflicts of interest which have to
be brought into tolerable harmony in any society. This is a
political problem with economic aspects. To achieve this harmony, self-interest has to be harnessed to social ends, and in
this process the automatic devices of the market have a part to
play, but subordinate to firm political and social controls. More-

over self-interest has to be balanced by a much firmer commitment to the common good; no 'divine hand' will automatically bring it about.

Both the market and the command economies present difficulties whether as ideal types or as they have worked out in practice. We are likely to live under some form of mixed economy which has to cope with the problems indicated in this lecture. Christians will hope to be a source of disinterested good will which the economic order certainly needs, but they also hope to shed some light, by the processes of reflection to which I referred at the beginning of this lecture, on how we can move towards a just and sustainable society, which is the theme of the third lecture.

— 3 —

Christianity and a Just and Sustainable Society

The title of this lecture is suggested by a current study programme of the World Council of Churches. Tribute is due to the remarkable recovery of Christian Social Ethics that has been made through the Ecumenical Movement. It goes back to what was known as the Life and Work side of that movement, dating from the Stockholm Conference of 1925. There was a major advance at the Oxford Conference of 1937 on 'Church, Community and State', against a setting in Europe of Nazi and Fascist totalitarian governments, and prolonged mass unemployment following upon the economic crash of 1929. Much of the theological work that went into the Oxford Conference is still relevant. So is that which went into its successor at Geneva in 1966 a generation later. By then the horizon had become global.

The sub-title of the Geneva Conference on Church and Society was 'Christians in the Technical and Social Revolutions of our Time'. This could fairly be said to be the most thoroughly ecumenical conference ever held in the history of the Christian church. All the main Christian confessional traditions were well represented. Roman Catholic participant observers played an active part; several had been involved in the preparation of the Pastoral Constitution of the Second Vatican Council, *Gaudium et Spes*.[1] The accession to the World Council of Churches in 1961 of the Russian and other Orthodox churches from Eastern Europe meant that the orthodox representation was much increased. The membership was so arranged that those who came from the Third World countries were sufficiently

numerous to be influential and not be made part of a process
and an agenda that reflected the preoccupations of the 'Christian'
West. Moreover lay folk were as numerous as clergy; and many
of them were highly competent in their occupations. It is significant that the result of a conference set up in this way proved
radical, so radical that many Christians from the 'established'
churches were disturbed by it, though in retrospect it does not
seem so fearful now. Indeed its concerns have moved steadily
more into the forefront ever since. However it was a study conference and not an executive one, so the question was, When the
next Assembly of the World Council of Churches met in 1968 at
Uppsala, would the official representatives of the churches en-
dorse the conclusions reached at Geneva two years previously
or take fright and repudiate them? In fact they broadly accepted
them. The result was a development of the Geneva themes in a
subsequent study which culminated at a conference in Bucharest
in 1974 under the title, 'Science and Technology for Human
Development: the Ambiguous Future and the Christian Hope'.
This in turn reported to the most recent Assembly of the World
Council of Churches at Nairobi in 1975.

The greater part of this work has been the responsibility of
the Department on Church and Society of the World Council of
Churches. It has had to respond to varied emphases and pressures in a global context, and with vast problems which have
shown further ramifications as they have been investigated. The
most complex of these has been the ethical issues involved in the
development of nuclear energy. The Department has pursued
an excellent method of interdisciplinary study involving experts
from various disciplines working with theologians and those of
practical experience, often from situations of intense difficulty
and conflict. It has been clear that its role is not to try and speak
for the churches, but if possible to speak *to* them, in the hopes of
briefing them in such a way that by having the relevant information sifted and the range of ethical issues explored, they will
be in a better position to respond to what is actually happening
rather than to what they may imagine to be happening.[2] The
upshot is that for the first time in centuries the churches have

available some organized thought on social issues which is up to date to guide them. If they persist in archaic attitudes it is a wilful persistence.[3]

The Bucharest Conference revealed how much still needed to be done, so it was no surprise that the Nairobi Assembly decided to continue the work, and a well prepared major world study conference is due in the USA in July 1979 under the over-all title 'Faith, Science and the Future'. Its sub-title is more informative: 'The Contribution of Faith, Science and Technology in the struggle for a Just, Participatory and Sustainable Society'. The term 'participatory' was a later addition to 'just' and 'sustainable' and is in my opinion unnecessary, since if people are not allowed to participate in decision-making in their own society it can hardly be called a just one. In exploring the theme of this lecture I shall refer to some of the exploratory ecumenical material, but before doing so I return to the legacy of the Christian thinking on capitalism and socialism.

I

The discussion in the first lecture centred on a critique of what we might call the general philosophy of capitalism, together with some reflections on the extent of the past and possible future influence of religion (meaning the Christian religion in the context of this discussion) on the economic and social order. The second lecture was chiefly concerned with capitalism and socialism, or market and command economies, considered both as ideal types and in the ambiguities they show in practice. Christian socialist critics of capitalism have gone on to produce criticisms of the basic structures of capitalism which must be mentioned briefly. They have not been cogent, and it is not difficult in the light of our previous discussions to see why. The most common criticism is to say that production should be for use and not profit. This ignores the problem of deciding which among all the things we might produce with our relatively scarce resources should be produced. Profit is an excellent criterion for deciding, for it indicates what in fact those who buy the product do consider to be so useful that they should be produced, always provided that the profit mechanism is put within a much wider and tougher social framework than enthusiasts for *laissez-faire* allowed for.

Again Christian socialists have felt uneasy about competition itself, as setting man against man instead of providing a structure within which man co-operates with man. The motive of service is contrasted with the motive of self-interest seeking for profit. The report of a World Council of Churches Consultation in 1978, held as part of the preparation for the 1979 Conference, says in two places that social concern should be the motive for production and basic economic activity.[4] However no society can be so ordered that it can depend solely on the motive of service. Self-interest has to be harnessed. It is too powerful, persistent and indeed necessary to be ignored. This is not only for ignoble reasons, but because of concern for that most basic unit of society, the family. Furthermore no one is good or wise enough to decide for other people how they can best make their contribution to society. Persons must be allowed wide scope to make that decision for themselves. Nevertheless self-interest must not be exalted above all other motives in life, such as the desire to be useful and respected, or the desire to exercise authority and leadership by those who have managerial and entrepreneurial skills. It must also be tempered by built-in structures of resistance by other individuals and groups, and by the law. Just as fundamental is the need to temper it by the cultivation of a concern for the common good, the element of 'disinterested goodwill' whose necessity Bryan Wilson has stressed, as I mentioned in the first lecture.

'The common good' is a term referred to frequently in Roman Catholic social teaching, though it is not by any means exclusive to it, and is suspect by some as calling for a reverent resignation towards social inequalities which ought to be remedied, and towards hierarchies which ought to be questioned.[5] It is true that Christians do have a persistent tendency to call for co-operation and 'pulling together' in a way that assumes there are no fundamental conflicts of interest. But there is no necessity for this. A commitment to the common good does not rule out that the best realization of it at a particular moment may be the outcome of conflict. What it does mean is that conflicts must be carried out within an overarching awareness that while my personal or group interests must be represented, heard and allowed for, there are other interests which I am not likely to be as forcefully aware of as my own (still less is my group likely to be as aware of the interests of other groups). These also have to be considered. No assumption is made that the interests are equally cogent. They may be, or some may have little or no cogency. But they must be represented, and out of the tussle in the public forum an approximation to the common good must be sought. We all need an awareness that there is an interest greater than our own interest, a good greater than our own good. Without it the political and economic forum becomes nothing but a ferocious struggle between persons and groups who can see nothing but their own cause and write off their adversaries with a good conscience. This sense of the common good does not depend on explicit religious belief, but it is a concept which Christians should specially be concerned to contribute to the body politic, and to foster in co-operation with those of other faiths and ideologies in a plural society.

The Christians who made these over-simple criticisms of capitalism tended to equate the concept of the kingdom of God in the gospels with an ideal society, a socialist or co-operative commonwealth, to which with varying emphases they thought society is evolving and humanity is called to build. This was one aspect of what was known, particularly in the USA, as the 'social gospel'. It seems now entirely to have disappeared under the influence of New Testament criticism, which has shown conclusively that the kingdom of God in the teaching of Jesus is not a future social order, but a radical present and future eschatological presence which challenges any social order as it transcends any. This is a substantial point gained. It is noteworthy that even the most revolutionary-minded Latin American Liberation theologians are saying that however necessary it is for Christians to be committed to revolution, they will need to bring a theological critique to bear on the post-revolutionary society.

The mistake made by the Christian criticisms I have just been discussing was to move too directly from some basic New Testament concept or some doctrinal position to a specific conclusion on the structures of the economic order, like profit and the competitive market. The connection between the Christian faith and the social order is profound but less direct than this. Even the Liberation theologians agree on this. They use a Marxist analysis of the economic order because they have persuaded themselves that it is in fact, as Marxists claim, 'scientific' in the sense of being a reliable basis for action. They do not get it from the Bible or any other Christian source. According to them these latter provide the motivation for action whilst Marxism provides the analysis on which to act.

Christianity is always in search of an economic order through which to express itself. It cannot simply say that socialism is the economic expression of Christianity. In so far as socialism is a utopian 'from each according to his ability, to each according to his needs', it is an inspiring vision beyond empirical realization, and it is as impossible to move from it directly to immediate decisions in the economic order as it is to base them directly on the New Testament concept of the kingdom of God. In so far as the term socialism refers to existing socialist economies, they exhibit ambiguities which cry out for theological as well as political and economic critiques. Still less can capitalism be said to be the economic expression of Christianity; only the belief in the 'divine hand' ever gave that view plausibility. Capitalism relies explicitly far too exclusively on self-interest, ignoring the necessity of other motives on which (as we have seen) it must implicitly rely in practice but does nothing to cultivate, and indeed actually undermines. On the other hand socialist theorists, whether Christian or secular, have tended to work with an over-optimistic view of man which assumes that it is only because of capitalism that self-interest is so powerful; change to socialist structures and it will disappear, together with the conflicts of interest which go with it.[6] Hence they have been too sanguine about the concentration of economic and political power in the same hands in command economies, and of the need to provide checks on the abuse of power. Once this is seen some socialists, again both Christian and secular, are tempted to avoid the problem of power by talking of small, manageable, local units which are run by common consensus. If 'participatory' means this it is a delusion. Power has to be central as well as local. It has to be used; it also has to be open to check against abuse. Consensus is admirable, where it can be achieved and achieved in time; but the possibility of minorities remains, and they must have means of calling in question abuses of power by majorities.[7]

It will be evident from this discussion that I do not think that the collapse of some of the traditional arguments against capitalism means the collapse of the entire Christian critique. It is true that this critique applies to any social order and not only capitalism, but it does suggest a radical presumption which calls into question a good deal of what is actually going on in market economies. It advances a range of considerations, which in turn leaves open a range of options by which the economic order might better meet these considerations than it does at the moment. The most important of these considerations include the following.

1. A concern for the poor and unprivileged. This is fundamental in the Judaeo-Christian tradition, though it has often been neglected or interpreted narrowly and paternalistically.

2. A conviction that the basic equality of all men in the sight of God, and the belief that Christ died for all, is more fundamental than the things in which they are unequal. This fundamental equality has to find expression in the structures of society so that men will feel at home with one another. A corporate sense of human togetherness is fundamental to Christianity and calls into question an individualist philosophy.[8]

3. The Christian understanding of man sees that his dignity requires that he should participate in decisions which affect him as a worker and a citizen, and his sinfulness requires that

there should be checks on the abuse of power because no one is good enough to exercise power over others with no possibility of check.

4. The Christian doctrine of the state emphasizes not only its negative role of restraining disorder but its positive role of creating and encouraging social institutions, structures and conventions which facilitate rather than hinder the living of the good life (in the sense of 1, 2 and 3).

When Christians realize that there is not a simple Christian critique of capitalism, and also that there are no in-built moral or technical factors which lead us to suppose that current market economies are going necessarily to break down, they tend to become silent on the social and economic order and to return to concentrating on the old evangelical stress on personal motivation. Motivation is obviously important, as far as it goes. For instance Christians, in common with other men, must have a concern for justice, and it is quite possible that Christians can give a much firmer motivation to the search for justice than can be given on a purely secular basis. Efforts to establish a rational basis for the pursuit of justice, such as John Rawls' notable study, *A Theory of Justice*, are extremely important, but it is hard to believe that they will provide a sufficient motivation without some greater dynamic than can come from the kind of rational contractual political analysis which Rawls attempts. Moreover Christians should give thought to the role of motivation, because an unreflecting form of Christianity can lead, and has often led, to complacency in social attitudes on the one hand or to fanaticism on the other, including a nationalism which at times is little better than tribalism. A more thoughtful form of Christian motivation should give greater insights into these failures, and more stamina to pursue the cause of justice without the necessity of being given utopian hopes before one can be galvanized into action. When these hopes are disappointed there is a danger of a lapse into quietism. But to concentrate on motivation is not enough. Christians still need to work at educating themselves to make more responsible and informed specific decisions in their work and as citizens; and churches need to continue to reflect carefully and corporately on the lines of policy they are going to advocate.

In this process of reflection two general questions are currently raised which are not easily resolved. The first is, What is to be the attitude of the Christian to relative affluence? The second, What is to be his attitude to nature? At first sight there is the most astounding contrast between the relative affluence of our society and the presuppositions of the New Testament and the relative poverty of the world out of which it came. The New Testament contains many dramatic warnings against the danger of riches. However I do not see that these warnings necessarily carry the corollary that there is something admirable about either physical or mental drudgery in itself, though equally there is nothing demeaning about physical and mental drudgery where it is necessary for the common good. If this kind of servile physical and mental labour can be prevented and human beings released from it for more creative activities, not least to enjoy the creation whilst not abusing it, there seems no reason to cavil.[9] Certainly relative affluence enlarges the possibilities of choice through the range of human contacts and communications, as well as the greater material resources it puts at man's disposal. The sting in the New Testament references is to riches in the midst of poverty. This is the sting that the relatively prosperous First, Second and Third (oil) Worlds now have to face in respect of their relations to the vast Fourth World. Provided this is taken to heart, and I realize it is a big proviso, there seems no reason why on Christian grounds we should repudiate relative affluence. At the same time we should be aware that there is value in those elements in the Christian faith which lead to the renunciation of wealth as a warning against its dangers, notably a restless thirst for novelties, a wish to show off, and a desire for ever greater accumulation of wealth. It is here that alternative life-styles of varied kinds, whether practised by groups or individuals, can have an important role.[10]

What is to be the attitude of Christians to nature? The ecologists have been criticizing the Christian faith as one of the sources of an exploitative attitude to nature by Western man. There are large issues here, which I have dealt with on another occasion,[11] and can do no more now than say that we must maintain a theology which goes from God to nature via man and not to nature direct. We must maintain that nature is to be ruled by man under God, that is to say under God for men, as a loving response to God's creative and redeeming activity. The Judaeo-Christian faith has emancipated man from a monism which merges him in nature and which leads to quietism and a rationalization of privileges. We must not be stampeded by the recent agitation, nor by the examples of brash over-confidence which must be admitted, into abandoning a proper sense of man's authority over nature, otherwise nature will soon swamp him.

II

I turn now to an appraisal of the ecumenical work on a just and sustainable society, remembering that it is in progress and not complete. If men have a common humanity to link them together it is not difficult to see that they have certain basic needs in common, such as the need for food (calories, proteins), housing, sanitation, clothing, household goods, health care (especially to ensure low infant mortality). Broadening out from these very basic needs we come to needs which are more directly related to the quality of life than merely sustaining it; for instance transport and education (literacy). Going beyond these there are the needs for a truly 'human' form of community life, of creativity, of variety, of participation in decision-making in one's own circumstances, in short the need to live in structures which work in a humane and just way, and not structures which actually tempt and play on human weaknesses. It has been said that a 'Christian' social order is one whose structures require bad people to do good things, as distinct from making good people do bad ones. In more abstract terms one can refer to a just society as involving equality in respect of basic freedoms, basic order to secure basic security, and ways of handling change which are both efficient and humane. There is no theory,

Christian or other, which is capable by itself of producing a reasonable compromise between these different considerations, still less of eradicating possible contradictions between them. It has to be a matter of empirical judgment from time to time, taking the best information that is possible on the current problems and the possible ways of solving them.

The basic problem to my mind is that of equality. If a just society is to be thought of as one in which everyone can grow to his full maturity, and not only the top two-thirds, then equality cannot just mean meritocracy, or an equal start in competing for scarce rewards; it must go deeper than that. It must include not only a provision of basic needs but also of the right of all to participate in decision-making, not only politically in their capacity as citizens but also in their job as workers. As is well known, a vigorous consideration of this last point, which has been latent for a long time, is at last smouldering. Little progress has been made so far, but it is an issue which will not die down and must be more vigorously pursued. The managerial side of industry is hesitant and fearful, and the workers' side divided because it is afraid·that accepting some managerial responsibility will impede the full representation of its interests as against those of the managers and consumers. Yet not to grasp this nettle is as degrading to the workers as is acquiescence in a system of payment by tipping.

The requirements of a just society are more moral ones, whilst the requirements of a sustainable society are more technical ones. I think that the term 'sustainable' is better than the alternatives that are being used such as 'the steady state society' or 'the zero growth society or 'the equilibrium state society', all of which are less flexible in their connotation than the term 'sustainable'. I say this even though I know that many who use the word 'sustainable' do in fact use it in a rather inflexible way. On the other hand it can be used in a general way. The Zurich report defines it as one 'in which the number of people, the rate of use of resources and the rate of pollution of the biosphere are within the capacity of the earth to support'. This requirement is one which should certainly be accepted, but meeting it could fall far short of what I, or this report as a whole, would regard as just.

Clearly much more work needs to be done on this concept. In the preparatory studies five general criteria and three recommendations concerned with a just and sustainable society have been mentioned.[12]

1. The demand for food must be kept below the global capacity to supply it. This seems sensible enough, but it does not help us much when we remember that on a world scale the productivity of agriculture is great. The problem is, apart from creating reserve stocks for contingencies, to get the food where it is wanted and to create effective demand for it where it is wanted, rather than any danger that the limits of food supply are likely to be reached. If ten per cent of the extra skill of the most efficient farmers, for instance the Danish, could be transferred to the vast mass of still inefficient farmers, there would be no worries about possible food supplies.

2. The use of non-renewable resources should not outrun the increase of resources secured through technical innovation. This again seems sensible, but it loses much of its force when it is realized that it is the threatened running out of resources which is the chief stimulant to the technical effort and motivation needed to discover both more resources, and methods of using existing resources more efficiently.

3. There should be no emission of pollutants beyond the capacity of the earth to absorb them. This is obviously right. We need a less polluting technology. As we have already noted, the technical innovations made possible after the last war by the technical developments during the war meant that our technical capacities outran our monitoring techniques, so that there has been serious danger of over-pollution of earth, air and water. Fortunately once this is realized it is not in principle difficult to deal with, nor is it terribly expensive in terms of the extra resources required to do so. On the other hand developing countries tend to think that concern with pollution is a luxury that they cannot afford; but they

must be asked whether they are not over-sanguine in this respect.

4. We should feel responsibility at least for our grandchildren. This raises the question of how far we are indeed responsible for the future. My answer would be to the extent that we are able reasonably to look ahead in the matter in question. In many cases this will not be much more than about fifteen years, which is as long as anyone looks ahead if he discounts the future at a rate of ten per cent per annum. Yet this is a good deal longer than the interval beween general elections in this country, which tends too much to be the limit which politicians have in mind. In some matters we should indeed look ahead to the time of our grandchildren, but it is a hazardous undertaking, far less certain than those who talk pretentiously of futurology admit. On the question of radio-active nuclear waste, however, we are dealing with an altogether different time dimension, and it raises technical and ethical issues which require, and are beginning to get, full discussion.[13]

5. The level of human activity should not cause adverse effects on the global climate. I pass this by because the evidence seems to me to be so tenuous and the horizons so distant that it is impossible to say anything of present significance about it.[14]

Then there are three more specific recommendations on the achieving of a just and sustainable global society.

1. There should be a stable population in both rich and poor countries. This is not self-evident. It is certainly true that rates of growth need considering, especially in lands where they can produce a doubling of the population in fifteen years, but that is not the same thing as saying that a stable population is required. More thought needs to be given to this.

2. For rich countries a reduced rate of growth, or no growth rate or an actual reduction in living standards is suggested. They should concentrate on the quality of life rather than on the quantity of goods and services. Maximum levels of consumption should be set and not exceeded. In poor countries

more growth is held to be necessary, as well as an appropriate technology and the achieving of a minimal level of consumption. Just as the developing societies are afraid of pollution controls, so they are afraid of the 'small is beautifull, line on technology, lest it should be a means of depriving them of useful technological developments which the wealthy take for granted and wish to deny the poor. (They are also afraid of population controls.) They are not wise on any of these issues, but it is not easy for anyone from the wealthy world to convince them of this.[15] They are also beginning to talk the language of self-reliance and of detaching themselves from the economic giants.[16] It is easy to see why. They want to be free from the ties of what they call neo-colonialism. However it is not yet clear from the study material how self-reliance is to relate to the necessary and proper interdependence of peoples in the world.[17] The wealthy could also begin to detach themselves, and self-reliance is no gospel for the richer parts of the world; it would be an invitation to selfishness.

3. We should move to a trans-national social security system, a kind of welfare world and not merely a series of welfare states for the more fortunate. This is an admirable suggestion, easy to state though complex to work out; every step towards it will take a long and hard political effort. A contribution can be made by the EEC as it considers the applications of Spain, Portugal and Greece to join it.

III

Although more work is needed on the just and sustainable society, it already presents a challenge to the rich countries and the churches in them which further work is not likely to remove. The challenge is there although in my judgment too much in the criteria and recommendations reflects the influence of the ecological and the 'limits to growth' type of thought, which assumes the incapacity of our physical environment to support a much higher level of production and consumption than it does today. I have already said that there are good reasons to suppose that this is a mistake. Allied with this is the thought that the rich segments of the world have reached a material level of living which, if continued, will harm the quality of life in the poorer parts of the world. That is to say that the over-all quality of life will be increased by material growth among the poor, and either very limited growth, or stability, or a reduction (the language varies), in the consumption of the rich. In fact both could grow together, as has been happening for some time, including the years 1973 to 1977. But will they continue to do so? That depends very much on the behaviour of the rich, whose priorities in the use of their wealth needs to change. To say this may seem like letting the rich off the hook, and maybe it will do so, but one cannot disguise the truth of the matter for fear that the rich will misuse their strong position.

It is because of an unwillingness to admit this that some of the language of the ecumenical study is over-dramatic. We are told that a new social order which is just and sustainable must emerge if catastrophe is to be avoided, and that there is less than a generation to create the transition if humanity is to survive. The impulse behind such a statement is not so much cogent evidence to support it as moral indignation which assumes that what is unjust ought to, and therefore will, collapse.[18] This obscures the capacity of injustice to survive. It obscures the fact that the danger is that the wealthy countries of the world will be content to live in a global slum. It is doubtful if the tactics of the OPEC countries with respect to oil can be used in respect of any other commodity needed by the wealthy, whether copper or aluminium or phosphorous or uranium. In my view the rich nations, if they chose to take an economically isolationist stance, could organize themselves on an available resource base which they could sustain for generations. To assume that they could not is once again to assume that what is morally wrong will necessarily collapse. This is true in the long run, but the long run may be a long one indeed; and in that long run, as Lord Keynes said, we are all dead. It is hardly relevant to decision-making in the present. I think that the wealthy countries will move steadily towards knowledge industries, like data processing, and still more into the realm of services, and that more manufacturing industry, as well as intermediate technology and improved agricultural techniques, will be characteristic of less developed and only just developing countries. This will not happen quickly. For instance, the wealthy countries will continue to adjust fairly slowly, propping up relatively inefficient industries and relatively high-cost agriculture, but this is what the tendency will be.

There is no example of a civilization voluntarily withdrawing from an advantageous position, and therefore it is unrealistic to put some of these proposals to the wealthy without realizing that they have to be shown that their long-term interest is the same as that of the developing countries. We must of course appeal to their idealism, not least because so many of the wealthy nations have a Christian tradition, but we must also search for ways of showing the unpleasant political consequences to them in the kind of world that will result if they pay no attention to the needs of the poor It is an absolute crucial question: How is the wealthy West going to use its wealth? My estimate is that after the brief check to growth we are now experiencing, our Gross National Product will continue to grow, in the next decade and after that, at an average rate of about 3% per annum. What are we going to do about our own unprivileged? The old, the low-paid, the handicapped and above all the unemployed (to whom I shall return in a minute). What policies of trade and aid are we going to work for and implement with respect to the Fourth World? This is the test of our comparative wealth. A new international economic order is even more of a political problem than an economic one.

The challenge to churches in the Zurich study is to establish an appropriate asceticism, a voluntary life-style for committed Christian peoples. It is one that should be not *other*-worldly, like the spurious kind of piety which has so often been exposed in the past, nor *inner*-worldly, like the Protestant asceticism of power, work and thrift, but *pro*-worldly – that is to say, one which takes this world seriously and enjoys it, but is concerned not to use an unfair share of it, and to work for the fair access of all to the good things in it. The study makes a plea for Christian pilot communities, oddly enough with a strong rural base. It is not clear to me why this is said, since it ignores the predominant and growing urbanization of life in so many parts of the world, developing and developed countries alike. Christian pilot communities in an urban society would seem at least as important. The whole theme of what alternative communes can and cannot achieve is a separate issue; they are not an alternative to the task of organizing better over-all political and economic structures, but their indirect influence may be great. Certainly there is the need for radical and experimental groups within the Christian church.[19]

How do these challenges bear on the United Kingdom? We must never forget the poverty and misery still existing in large parts of the world, in such sharp contrast to the affluence of the society to which I belong. Robert McNamara, the president of the World Bank, referred starkly in a speech in 1975 to the nine hundred millions suffering from absolute poverty, in the sense of squalor, hunger, hopelessness and low life expectancy. But we cannot translate our situation into a different one. It seems to me that if we in the United Kingdom resolutely tackle our own problems in terms of a just and sustainable society we are much more likely to make the right contribution towards such a global society, and not merely one for the wealthy West.

If we are going to take the needs of the unprivileged seriously we have a major problem on our own doorsteps. What are we going to do about the unskilled unemployed manual worker? At the moment we have one and a half million unemployed in this country, and at least a third of these are under twenty-five. In the EEC about one in twenty of those who want work cannot find it. They come predominantly from the unskilled manual workers and, among them, particularly from the various minority groups. This is not due solely to a temporary trade recession, but is also a matter of long-term structural change. There will be fewer and fewer jobs for the unskilled in our society. Yet we cannot tolerate a considerable minority of our community being regarded as unwanted. If we do we shall bring social disasters upon our own heads. People must feel that what gifts they have are wanted by the community, which must find a way of calling upon them.

If this is taken seriously it will mean a long-term shift in many attitudes and values in our society. I give three examples.

1. We shall have to adopt a much less arduous attitude to work, and the cultivation of a sense of the value of leisure without any accompanying sense of guilt; perhaps this could mean a secularization of the contemplative life characteristic of the Catholic tradition, to modify the secularized Protestant work ethic.

2. It requires a new attitude to differentials, especially in relation to reducing the more and more frustrating individual scramble for positional goods which Professor Hirsch has analysed and which I discussed in the second lecture.[20] It might well involve a basic wage, not very different whether one is employed or not, and an emphasis on meeting social needs, especially in calling on the services of the young in the community. At the moment various key groups are pursuing their own interests and thinking little about the common good, whether they be airline pilots, civil servants, doctors and those of other professions, or key workers in manufacturing industries. It is not that groups should refrain from representing their interests. Each group knows more of how things appear to it than the rest of us do, but if a complex participatory democracy is to work, this representation must be laced with a strong sense of the common good within which disputes must be settled before the bar of public opinion. This itself has the obligation of weighing issues, and especially being alert to those who have the least industrial power.

3. A further change of attitude is also required because of the increased wages of those who are at work, bringing into the net large numbers of people who hitherto have not paid income tax; they are showing the same reluctance to pay taxes that has been characteristic so long of the middle

classes. This attitude must change if we are to enjoy more collective provision of positional goods. Therefore to deal with the problem of the unemployed manual worker will involve in the course of the next decades a considerable reconstruction of our attitudes to the whole of social and economic life.

The churches will have to think carefully about the kind of lead they give collectively. As an example of the possibilities of one kind of lead they might give I refer to a study of the 895 candidates at the elections to the General Synod of the Church of England in 1975,[21] compared with an earlier survey of a weighted cross-section of the British population surveyed for the 1966 general election by Butler and Stokes. (Almost 70% of the respondents claimed nominal membership of the Church of England.) What has emerged so far in sifting the evidence is, first, the overwhelmingly middle-class nature of the General Synod candidates, and second, that their attitudes by no means always echo that of their class or the general public. 99% described themselves as middle-class (and 79% were upper-middle-class in the sense of belonging to class A and B of the usual market research Heads of Households classification). The investigation included an examination of their attitudes to three prominent issues compared to standard middle-class attitudes. The first was whether they were against further nationalization; 78% of the Synod candidates said they were, as compared with 85% of the general middle class. The second was whether they were against the abolition of the death penalty; 22% of the Synod candidates said they were, as against 77% of the general middle class. The third was whether they thought there were already too many immigrants in this country; 29% of the Synod candidates said that they thought so, as against 80% of the general middle class. This shows that on their attitude to nationalization the Synod candidates were very similar to that of the middle class as a whole, but on the other two issues they were vastly different. I should say they were more far-seeing than the general attitude of the middle class in the country and,

I may add, still more so than the general attitude of the working class. Many middle-class sympathizers with the Labour movement find it most disconcerting how on questions of differentials, or on such questions as immigration, the death penalty, and other matters, working-class opinion is far from what could be called progressive. It would be fascinating to speculate why these figures turn out as they do, but the only lesson I draw for the moment is that it is not unrealistic to expect that those who are in the leadership of the churches may, if they wish, exercise a distinctive role of leadership in opinion-forming in the country, and that there is no necessary reason to suppose that they will only echo conventional middle-class opinions.

IV

In reflecting on the persistence of capitalism Christians can sympathize with, but also call into question, elements from all the main political traditions in this country. As far as the Left is concerned its equalitarian and communal strands are very congenial to a Christian understanding of man in community; but Christians will call into question the utopian elements in its thought, especially the idea that human beings are almost infinitely malleable, so that all one has to do is to arrive at the right structures in which to put them and then all will be well. Christians will also find the libertarian side of the Radical tradition congenial, and also its emphasis on rationalism, for the cultivation of irrationality is no way to honour God. But they will disagree with the individualism which has also been so widespread in that tradition; indeed the word 'person' is more congenial to them than the word 'individual'.[22] Christians can also enter appreciatively into the organic elements in the political traditions of the Right, but they will not approve of the traditions of privileges and paternalism which have gone with it; nor will they allow the Right to monopolize a philosophy of human imperfection, for properly understood it calls into question policies of the Right as it does those of the Left.[23]

However it does not follow that because their faith can both support and call into question strands in differing political traditions Christians can adopt an uncommitted attitude on the touchline. That is in fact tacitly to side with things as they are, not least because the issues of the persistence of capitalism and various socialist alternatives in the end prove to be more political than economic.

Because the issues are complex and because we have more power to decide them and more people wanting to have a say in the decisions, it is important that Christians should not abandon the political task. They will need a renewed grasp of the insights of their faith, though they will make more modest claims for it in so far as it bears on the details of economic, industrial and political life. Nor can they be effective in a plural society without allies. Nevertheless the Christian faith is the source both of spiritual strength and of critical insights which can be brought alongside the expertise and insights of others in the search for a just and sustainable society. It can be a powerful influence in producing the disinterested goodwill looked for by Bryan Wilson and the commitment to moral values which Professor Hirsch has shown to be necessary for a healthy social order. Of the three sources of sustenance for these values to which Professor Hirsch referred, traditional social ties, religious teaching and a sense of civic duty, he could only see much strength in the last. This is the one which the Chinese are strenuously fostering in the hopes of eradicating all anti-social attitudes by intensive life-long education in suitable social structures almost from the cradle, so that in fifty years their revolution will be secure. I have expressed sympathy for this, though I think it has illusions built into it. In a Christian view man is more than a citizen and has an eternal destiny, even though he cannot be saved alone. A perspective on society from this point of view, which accepts man's corporateness but yet presents him with a challenge and a vision from beyond his society, is the best hope of preserving the civic virtues from corruption, and living with the provisionality of politics. In our society Christianity has to foster the social virtues, which capitalism tacitly assumed but ignored and undermined, and the traditional social ties, so that the two together strengthen the sense of civic duty.

Technological, social and political forces have produced in advanced industrial countries societies in which change is endemic but which are not suited to revolutionary change, whether the revolution is violent or not. To avoid this the changes need to be made wisely and in time. We need to move to a society where the capitalist element is so much under social control that it no longer gives its name to the whole. That is why there must be an attack on the individualistic philosophy which primarily sets man against man as the mainspring of society. The number of radicals who genuinely hold it is small, and in practice it is taken over verbally by those of the political Right, who are the first to secure special interventions by tariffs, quotas and controls if they get the chance. The end result is to favour the powerful. The Right needs saving from itself in this respect. Men and women are meant primarily to live in communities of giving and receiving, some of us at one time doing more of the one and at another more of the other. What the church, however brokenly, exemplifies is a sign of what the plural society should express in its structures. Only within a framework which expresses this can self-interest be harnessed by such a very useful device as the free market, and competition be allowed to resolve impersonally basic economic problems of choice.

Whatever politicians say, there will be no escape from the political control of the essentials of economic policy. Big business units and organized labour have both now become so powerful in terms of fixing prices and wages that some kind of incomes policy has become inevitable, and we shall have to grope towards finding the right institutions to formulate it.[24] It is not, however, inevitable that we should work towards a lessening of differentials and the liquidation of particular inheritances in perhaps three generations, but I think we should. Whether and how far such a society should properly be called social democracy or democratic socialism in subsidiary. This is of course a profoundly un-Marxian remark. Whereas I can see the one shading into the other in various ways, others would see a total contradiction between them. Some on the Left say that, leaving aside allegations of the inevitable economic breakdown of 'welfare' capitalism, holders of power may acquiesce in some erosions of it but will never surrender the substance of it willingly. Nothing short of forceful revolution will shift them. It could be so if the Marxist thesis is right. I have been able only briefly to indicate why I think it implausible.[25] Some on the Right in their turn say that democratic socialism is unworkable because its zeal for equality prevents efficiency, breeds envy and is incompatible with liberty. Perhaps enough has been said to suggest that this is also implausible. Politicians tend to exaggerate their differences from their opponents.

If we are to work in the general direction I have been advocating it is important that the need for some new attitudes is not overlooked. Even economic growth, which all political parties favour at the moment, needs to be in a new perspective and for much wider purposes. Nor must we give it up too soon. Keynes thought that social capitalism would do its global job in one hundred years (given a 2% growth rate per annum). We have had nearly half of these. In a conference in 1977 at Houston, Texas, 'World Alternatives to Growth' (partly sponsored by the Club of Rome) the celebrated American 'futurologist' Hermann Kahn thought that another two hundred years are needed to reach a sustainable society. My estimate is that at any rate another hundred years of *disciplined* growth will be needed to break the primordial global poverty barrier, and it is on this that we should set our sights.

To achieve a participatory and flexible social framework for economic life, with greater justice and a less exploitative attitude, requires great political patience, skill, endurance and wisdom. What precise mixes can be involved in what is now a capitalist-socialist continuum it is impossible to say. There are likely to be several possible options, but all of them will need a radical attitude. We saw in the first lecture that whatever influence Christianity has had (and estimates of the extent of it differ), it has been both a conserving and a reforming one.

There has been, however, too much of the conserving and too little of the reforming. F. D. Maurice said that his mission was to the unsocial Christians and the unchristian socialists. We have to find the equivalent of that nineteenth-century remark for the late twentieth century, when we have had experience of modified welfare capitalism and of some forms of socialism; and where instead of the former 'Christendom' situation Christians now live in an increasingly plural society.

II

Dissertations

— 4 —

Capitalism, Socialism, Personal Freedom and Individualism[1]

I

The stress on personal freedom, often expressed in the term individualism, has been such a potent force in our culture in the last three centuries that there is perhaps the need to say a little more about it than was possible in the compass of the Maurice Lectures.

A discussion of personal freedom involves a position taken with respect to an ongoing philosophical and intricate debate on the question of the freedom of the will and determinism.[2] It is not possible to enter into it on this occasion, but I must take leave to assume, as I did in the Maurice Lectures, that to some extent human beings are originators of their actions, and are therefore properly subject to moral evaluation in the shape of praise or blame. Personal freedom in this sense is fundamental to man as a moral being and it is a presupposition of all the 'high' religions, not least the Judaeo-Christian faith.

The Maurice Lectures continued a Christian debate on capitalism, and so assumed belief in the supreme worth of the human person as 'made in God's image', even though that image is at the same time flawed by sin. The distinctively Christian gospel moves on from creation to the belief that God has graciously drawn near to us in Jesus the Christ, through whose whole ministry the paradoxical power of the kingdom (or rule) of God has been launched into the world as a source of 'remaking' the tarnished image of God in man, and of his continued renewal. In principle we are free in Christ to be what we have it in us to be. However in the Christian view there is another and equally important affirmation to be made about personal freedom and that is that it can only be realized as we grow together in the community of Christians to our full maturity in Christ. This new community is of universal range. The Greek New Testament is full of *syn*-words, stressing the togetherness of Christians with Christ and with one another.[3] The Christian faith therefore stresses not only the importance of each person but also of that person finding his personhood in a community of persons. There is both the personal responsibility of each to make and follow decisions made by an informed conscience,[4] and also the corporate responsibility of the church. How to relate these two in practice in the right way has proved difficult enough in the internal life of the church, as the strains and stresses of church history bear abundant witness. How much more difficult is it, therefore, when it comes to exercising personal and Christian responsibility in the 'secular' structures of life. Yet Christian theology is bound to maintain that what should hold true in the church should be the ultimate criterion for life in these structures.

The Christian debate on capitalism is a prime example of the problems involved in relating the Christian understanding of human life and destiny to the social, economic and political structures in which men perforce live; that is to say in relating the universal kingdom of God to the structures of the world. There are two kingdoms in which Christians live at the same time. How they have linked the two in practice, and how they have considered they ought to be related, is a main theme of Christian history.[5] The church has lived in and with many different structures at different times, and lives in many different ones today. She now usually lives in structures which include persons of different faiths and philosophies or ideologies, so that she has to seek a will of God for those structures which cannot presuppose that those who live in them are either believing or nominal Christians. Many Christians in the West are particularly conscious today of the existence in this sense of plural societies, though there are clearly still many in the

United Kingdom who have not understood it and hark back to a much more uniform 'Christendom' situation.

There is one point of great importance in Christian doctrine (although it is not always granted) in connection with a plural society. This is that the basic doctrines of the Christian faith, of love, forgiveness, atonement and renewal, take to a deeper level through Jesus Christ fundamental human experiences in every-day living. Adumbrations of them are found in human life everywhere. Appeal can therefore be made to these experiences even when their deeper significance in Christian terms is not known or not accepted; thus at a certain level they can be the basis for living together in a plural society.

In the Maurice Lectures this Christian understanding of life was brought to bear upon two economic systems, capitalism and socialism, considered both as ideal types and, to some extent, in their empirical manifestations in the late twentieth century. It involved a reciprocal relation between a faith stance and a 'secular' enquiry, letting one throw light on the other. In particular the concern for persons-in-community was not used as the basis for a blueprint of an ideal social order to which the label 'Christian' could be attached, but as the basis for a critique of the underlying philosophies or allegedly 'scientific' theories which have been used to validate market or command economies. It was also used as a critique of some of their empiri-cal manifestations today. This was in order to indicate the general directions in which Christians might try to influence them. Within this general direction there will be different desir-able options in different societies, and usually more than one desirable possibility within any one of them. At this point detailed policy discussions are required, and there may well be differences of opinion between informed Christians within their over-all agreement. The Maurice Lectures were not on this level of detail.

II

A main concern of the Maurice Lectures was to cast doubt on a common philosophy of capitalism. This consists in erecting the institution of the free market into a general social philosophy based upon an individualistic understanding of human life. According to this it is only by appealing to individual self-interest, through creating the social institution of the free market, that the common good can be achieved.[6] Against this I did not argue that the opposite is the case, that the common good can only be achieved by social institutions based upon the appeal to universalism, or altruism (as some Christian Socialists argue). My argument was that self-interest is a powerful and necessary element in human life which must be allowed for and harnessed, but that it is also a dangerous element which has to be handled with care. The free market, which depends on it, is for certain social and economic purposes the most useful instrument yet devised by man, but it needs to be set within a strong social framework; to turn its basis into an over-all ideological basis for society is precisely the wrong way to move. Human beings are capable of universalism and altruism as well as a concern for self-interest. The latter is usually the stronger and more immediate attitude, so the former needs more encouragement. It is degrading to their humanity for men and women to be involved in institutions which foster only the stronger motive and deny the weaker. They need to live in over-all structures which call upon both, but foster the weaker. To some extent this is what the welfare state tries to do. (The individualist's rejoinder is that it is doing good at someone else's expense.)

But is this to do enough justice to individualism, and to what are sometimes called the virtues of capitalism? I am not thinking at this point of the classic capitalist propensity to erect thrift into a major virtue, but of the stress on individualism, independence, standing on one's own feet and not being beholden to anyone. After all it is only a short step from the Christian stress on the worth and responsibility of every person, particularly emphasized in Puritanism,[7] to the particular institutions of representative democracy and 'one adult, one vote'. In the course of this short step a successful attack on effete privilege was mounted, intellectual and economic adventure encouraged, room found for dissent and nonconformity, and the final autonomy of the individual stressed. Much of this proved a school of virtue which has contributed noble ingredients to the life of the country, not least in disciplined, upright, responsible living which has often been more profound in practice than the theory in which it was expressed. Its roots were not only in some aspects of the Christian faith but also in Renaissance man, which in turn drew upon versions of classical humanism. It is the twin heritage of elements of Christian faith and classical culture which gave it such moral momentum and an influence which still persists, particularly among our more senior citizens.

Nevertheless this view of man ignored an aspect of such importance that it is less adequate to call it a half truth than to say it is fundamentally false. It ignored the fact that society is prior to the individual in that the social structures into which he is born profoundly influence a person before he knows about it and that, as we have seen,[8] the individualism itself works only if a commitment to the common good can be counted on. This commitment individualism has ignored in theory and in practice undermined.

The philosophy of the free market which was classically expounded by Adam Smith had its ancestry in the political philosophy and institutions of seventeenth-century England. What was the conception of the individual which emerged from it? Professor C. B. Macpherson of Toronto University has written a classic study of the philosophy of individualism from Hobbes to Locke,[9] in which he sums up the assumptions of individualism under seven heads.

1. What makes a man human is freedom from dependence on the wills of others.
2. Freedom from dependence on others means freedom from any relations with others except those relations which an individual enters voluntarily with a view to his own interests.
3. The individual is essentially the proprietor of his own person and capacities, for which he owes nothing to society.
4. Although the individual cannot alienate the whole of his property in his own person, he may alienate his capacity to labour.

5. Human society consists of a series of market relations.
6. Since freedom from the wills of others is what makes a man human, each individual's freedom can rightly be limited only by such obligations and rules as are necessary to secure the same freedom for others.
7. Political society is a human contrivance for the protection of the individual's property in his person and goods, and (therefore) for the maintenance of orderly relations of exchange between individuals regarded as proprietors themselves.

The substance of this is to set every individual on his own. He owes nothing to society and is not part of a larger whole; he is free and human by virtue of his sole proprietorship of his own purposes. And society is essentially a series of market relations.

These seven points could bear close analysis in order to distil the element of truth buried in them, particularly in the sixth point, but it is the essence of the matter that is my concern, and that is the denial of the interrelationship of person and community; of the dependence of persons upon each other as well as their independence from each other. One does not need to be a Christian theologian to see the folly of this. The whole development of sociology as a distinct intellectual discipline with many branches witnesses to the centrality of social roles, institutions and structures. Also psychology, which has worked cautiously towards a normative concept of the autonomous person in studying human growth and development, is now moved to go further and add the quality altruism to the concept of autonomy.[10] Yet the influence of the individualistic model is still powerful. Nevertheless some who have seen its inadequacies in practice have tried to extract from it a better basis for social obligation, the most considerable recent attempt being that of Professor John Rawls.[11] This still tries to base social obligation on what a rational but not altruistic person would choose if he were to work out the terms of a social contract which would enable him to maximize in society his purposes, assuming that in doing so he was under a 'veil of ignorance' of what position he would in fact occupy in society. Even so, Rawls has been attacked by his fellow American Robert Nozick from an even more rigorist statement of the same individualist position; he holds that no new rights emerge with the state, and any rights it has must derive from a voluntary transfer of rights which individuals have under anarchy.

In contrast to this, for centuries Christian theology has expressed in various ways the organic and corporate nature of human life. One of the most fruitful, which I take as an example because it is not as well known in this country as it ought to be, is the Reformation doctrine of the Orders of Creation.[12] It is a way of understanding theologically the fact that certain basic structures of life are not chosen by man but are found to go with the mystery of human life itself. There are four of them:

1. Marriage and the family. Some structure of relations between the sexes lies behind the birth of children (no society can allow sexual relations to be an unregulated free-for-all), and children are profoundly influenced by the structure of family life – for instance whether nuclear or extended – long before they are sufficiently self-conscious to realize the fact and take any responsibility in and for it.

2. The Economic Order. This arises from the fact of the division of labour as soon as the family unit ceases to be self-sufficient, if we can bring ourselves to imagine such a state. Children are profoundly influenced by the economic structures into which they are born long before they can take any responsibility for them. Consider, for instance, the difference between the free market economy in its early days and a feudal economy.

3. The Political Order, especially the state. (Not the nation, which is a very fluid concept.) Everyone is born under some political authority which profoundly influences him long before he can take responsibility for it.[13] Life strikes one very differently under the different types of society all called democratic – Parliamentary, Guided or Peoples'.

4. The Community of Culture. This is a less defined but all-pervasive reality. With human life goes cultural activity, including such things as clothes, furniture, hair styles. It can go from the profound to the meretricious. It is not possible to

be non-cultural; the question to face is the quality of the culture, for it profoundly affects a child long before he is self-consciously aware of it.

The point about the Orders of Creation is that they are prior to human decision. No one, no group, sat down to decide whether to construct the institution of the family or the state. They arrived with human life itself. We do not decide to become part of the Orders of Creation. We are part of them willy-nilly. We cannot escape from them. They are prior to our decision yet profoundly affect us from birth. They are, according to this way of thinking, divine structures which ensure the minimum of human co-operation to make human life possible. But we should not be satisfied with this minimum. The market economy gets very near to being such a minimum. Rather, their purpose under God is to create the conditions through which each may grow with his fellows towards their full maturity.

The Orders of Creation are found in vastly different empirical forms. And with the exception of the community of culture, they are power structures, organizing and containing the vitalities of life. However, as we experience them they are all flawed by sin, as is each one of us personally. The doctrine of the Orders has been interpreted, as have all Christian social concepts, too conservatively, so that the existing social, economic and political power structures have been held to be ordained by God in the form currently experienced.[14] For this reason Bonhoeffer abandoned the term Orders of Creation (especially because the Nazis introduced another and spurious order, Race) and referred instead to the Mandates, whilst Barth used the term Provinces.[15] But to interpret the Orders in this conservative fashion is a corruption of the doctrine. Because as children we inherit them in a flawed state we are intended to use our influence, as we grow in maturity and responsibility, to modify them so that the structures work in a more human way. *Semper reformanda* applies not only to the church but to the Orders of Creation as well, just because they have such a profound influence on the person and on human flourishing. That is why the frequent polarization by Christians of 'changing persons' against 'changing structures' is so beside the point. Both aims need to be pursued all the time.

III

Both a sociological analysis of human life and the doctrine of the Orders of Creation show the absurdity of the individualist philosophy often advanced as the rationale of market economy capitalism, but that does not mean that a corporate view of human life has no dangers of its own. Some organic views have stressed the dependence of human beings on others but in an hierarchical and paternalistic fashion. This is what makes the classical free market theorist uncomfortable with much of the Right's thinking and practice. It is only marginally better to him than the collectivist thought of the Left. Again for a period Roman Catholic social thinking stressed the principle of subsidiarity in such a way as markedly to favour the corporate state as experienced, for instance, in Mussolini's Italy.[16] It was only Paul VI who rid Papal thinking of this.[17] In essence, however, that principle stresses the sensible point that a truly human society requires not merely a central state with appropriate structures, but also a whole series of regional, local and communal organs and activities, and that a larger unit should not undertake what can be satisfactorily carried out by a smaller one.

Socialist thinking is of course essentially organic. Some forms of it lead in the end to a loss of the person because of the assumption that all conflicts of interest are resolved in a socialist society, so that the political authorities inherently carry mass approval (apart from the odd anti-social individual or group), in whatever way the expression of that approval is organized.[18] In this case the person is lost in the community. Overt and covert action on behalf of the 'individual' is then necessary, but it is dangerous and often individuals and groups show great courage in sustaining it. In reaction against this form of highly centralized command economy, some socialist thought has bordered on anarchism in the belief that it is only institutions imposed from above which occasion conflicts of interest. Others have found in Maoist China what until recently they thought

was a model. Certain of the advocates of a participatory society
in ecumenical discussions reveal similar tendencies. The impression is given that participation can always be direct and not
representative (because the unit of decision making will be
small enough); that the decisions will be made in time; and that
there will be no disagreements.[19] There is therefore no need to
worry about restraints on the power of majorities to ride rough-
shod over minorities because there will be no minorities. When
one considers the complexity of running a state, above all the
complex interlocked advanced industrial economies, such assumptions can only occur to the most utopian mind; and the
idea that the problem can be avoided by extreme decentralization in accordance with the 'small is beautiful' philosophy is
equally utopian. However there is no need for socialists to adopt
such unrealistic assumptions. Rather it is necessary to admit
that the need for the small and local has to be met as well as the
need for the large and more centralized, and that the requirement of participation has to be worked at appropriately at all
levels. Similarly institutions for handling the perennial con-
flcits of interest between consumers in general and producers of
particular goods and services, and between managers and
managed have to be devised. Political and economic tasks in
this respect cannot be separated.

Socialism varies all the way from the utopia of 'from each
according to his ability, to each according to his needs' to what
used to be called gas and water socialism. The command economies show considerable variety in handling their affairs, as for
instance between the USSR and Yugoslavia, whilst the forms of
what is sometimes called the social market economy also vary
very considerably. As nationalized bodies the Coal Board and
Thomas Cook are very different, and so are Producers' Co-
operates (with which Maurice was associated) and the much
larger Consumers' Co-operative movement (which is what most
people think of when they refer to 'the Co-op'). They all have to
be judged in terms of their economic efficiency in the use of
resources, together with the extent of their success in securing
the informed participation of all with an interest in the enterprise (not forgetting the consumers), and in establishing effective

power structures which are subject to check if the power is abused. Similar criteria apply to trade unions, for instance with respect to their rule books and system of elections, as they do to the much less public world of ownership and management.

IV

Problems of conflicts of interest, of efficiency, of the demand for participation in decision making, will not go away whether we are thinking within terms of a market or a command economy or a mixture of the two. The philosophy of individualism is pursuing a will o'-the-wisp. People are not willing to subject vital aspects of their lives to impersonal processes. They want to argue them out in the public forum and, if they think it necessary, to use active means of protest (such as strikes or non-co-operation). Governments in the years after the first world war found it impossible to return to policies which profoundly affected the lives of their citizens yet were regulated by the impersonal Gold Standard, and they would find a similar impossiblity if they tried today to implement policies of the purer monetarist kind. It is not sufficient to give every adult citizen a national and local vote; he wants to participate in decision making not only in politics but in the circumstances in which he earns his living. Efforts to make both more effective are matters of everyday discussion. Politically there is the development of community work and community action in this decade, and industrially there is the discussion focused in the Bullock Report[20] which reflects in part British reaction to a movement which began in West Germany in 1952, though it also has roots in the Labour movement in this country. The report has not been well received but the issues it raises remain. In terms of consumers there has been the slow growth of a more effective consumers' movement, both privately, for example the Consumers' Association, and publicly in such a body as the Community Health Councils.

No significant group is in practice willing to work within the pure individualist theory of the market economy. (In a thoroughgoing demand economy, on the other hand, there is little choice but to conform, though occasionally the government can be shaken by popular protest, as has for instance happened twice in Poland.) The whole Labour movement, in the broad sense of the Party, the Trade Unions and the Co-operative Movement, has arisen as a protest against individualism. But on the owner-ship and management side the tale is the same when it comes to practice, whatever theoretical gestures are made towards indivi-dualism. There are demands for tariffs, quotas, and direct government subsidies, as well as less open attempts to establish monopolies and oligopolies. Nor does there seem much less of personal freedom when the taxpayer replaces the shareholder as the residual legatee of the losses (or, if it is not too far-fetched to mention it, the possible profits) of the British Leyland Motor Corporation. But of course at this point it is necessary to point out once more that most of us are producers of some particular goods or services whose cause we want to advance or protect from decline, and at the same time we are consumers in general in which role we have a direct interest in the most efficient use of scarce resources. Our divided interests are reflected in the give and take of public discussion and the often uncertain steps of government policies.

Our mixed economy is commonly called a Welfare State. It presupposes that the over-all handling of the economy must be in government hands, and argument centres in the extent and detail of its control over particular sections of it. It provides a minimum level of subsistence for the citizen by right – the dis-tinction between the deserving and undeserving poor has almost disappeared in theory, though it persists in many public atti-tudes – and it has been achieved by taxation policies which to a large extent amount to a re-distribution of income within the working class. As the more highly paid workers are drawn more fully into the tax net there are signs among them of an increasing resistance to taxation which has long characterized the middle class. They want a steady growth in take-home pay plus the social services benefits, but dislike the necessary taxes which cut into take-home pay. The philosophies of individualism and social concern are at war with one another and the matter has to be argued out, for the Welfare State is far from having solved its problems. It has never implemented Beveridge's intention that the social insurance benefits should guarantee subsistence without means test supplementation. Also the number of means-tested benefits is such that a poverty trap is created when the tax threshold begins, and this in the case of a married man with two children is when he reaches only half the national average wage. Moreover by the Family Income Supplement scheme, begun in 1970, we have actually returned to the derided Speen-hamland system of 1795 by subsidizing earnings.

Our form of the mixed economy has therefore as much yet to achieve in terms of social welfare as it has in terms of participation in decision making in work situations, or in dealing with problems of technological change with its effect on work, unemployment and leisure. Attitudes are somewhat schizophrenic. At one moment we revert to the individualistic talk of 'scroungers', and are far more concerned at the small percentage of fiddles than we are at the low take-up of benefits. Behind this is the theory that the individual ought to be independent and not beholden to his society. On the other hand there is a slowly growing appreciation of our common responsibility for coping with common misfortunes and handicaps. The Welfare State has meant an enlarged freedom of choice for most (the Health Service being a signal example[21]), and has opened a way of bearing one another's burdens which the philosophy of individualism could only leave to the fitful whim of private charity.

Nevertheless with rights as citizens go duties. Since we all tend to be more conscious of our rights than our obligations, continued efforts have to be made to reinforce the sense of civic obligation and to create structures which encourage it. The philosophy of individualism gave this up and took the easy course of relying in theory solely on the mutual restraints made necessary by the rational pursuit of self-interest.[22] It was blind to the fact that in practice it presupposed other motives which it either ignored or undermined. For a while it could deceive itself that a divine hand would ensure that the pursuit of private interest would bring about the public benefit. That deception is no longer possible. In fact it produced gross inequalities of wealth and power, and hazards which individuals will not put up with. The philosophy of individualism is false and will not work. On the other hand the working out of a concern for persons-in-community in always reformable social structures, institutions and more informal conventions remains permanently valid. This should be no surprise to the Christian, for it is precisely what his faith would lead him to expect.

— 5 —

R. H. Tawney as a Christian Moralist[1]

I *The Man*

As there is no biography of Tawney, and as he was the last person to think of writing an autobiography, I begin with a brief account of his life and work.[2]

Richard Henry Tawney was born in Calcutta on 30 November 1880, his father being a distinguished Orientalist in the Indian Educational Service. He was sent to Rugby School and, on arrival at the station platform for his first term, met there another new boy, William Temple. They were to go through the school together, and on to Balliol College, and to remain lifelong friends. Tawney read Greats and took a second-class degree, but he showed an even more singular deviation from the expected in never proceeding to the MA (apparently on the ground that it is to be obtained merely by paying a fee), although he was to receive nine honorary doctorates from universities all over the world.

Edwardian Britain was a land of deep social and political division and bitterness, and this made its mark on Tawney. In 1903 he followed in the track of a number of socially conscious upper-middle-class products of the ancient universities at the time, and went to live for two years at Toynbee Hall in the East End of London. He was Secretary of the Children's Country Holiday Fund. After this he became a teaching member of the Executive Committee of the newly formed Workers' Educational Association, and in 1907 an Assistant to the Professor of Political Economy at Glasgow University. At this time there took place at week-ends his famous WEA classes at Rochdale and at Longton in the Potteries; many of the cotton operatives in the former were said by the Master of Balliol to be worth first-class degrees. The classes were sponsored by Oxford University and were virtually the initiation of the University Tutorial Class System.[3] Temple, too, was to take a lifelong interest in the WEA, and Tawney and he together with their friend Albert Mansbridge, who founded it, formed a powerful triumvirate in it. Tawney was a member of the Executive Committee continuously from 1905 to 1940 and President from 1928 to 1943. In 1914 there was the interruption of war service. He returned to his work in adult education in 1919 as Oxford's first Resident Tutor in North Staffordshire. From 1918 to 1921 he was a Fellow of Balliol. Then came the move to the London School of Economics, where he was to remain until he retired, holding the Chair of Economic History in London University from 1931 to 1949.

In the first world war Tawney enlisted as a private, refused a commission, and rose to the rank of sergeant in the Manchester Regiment. On 1 July 1916 he was seriously wounded in the stomach in the advance of the Somme. (His essay *The Attack* gives a brilliant account of the episode.) Recovering in an army hospital in Oxford he was visited by Bishop Gore, who told the Matron as he left that she had one of the most valuable lives in England under her care. The Matron thereupon hurried to Tawney's bed and said, 'Why ever didn't you tell us you were a gentleman?'

Out of hospital Tawney was soon involved in public affairs. In 1919 he was a member of the Sankey Commission on the Coal Industry. It took another world war to implement its report. The industry remained a major concern of Tawney, and miners' welfare something to which he gave a lot of time. He was for years a 'back room' adviser of the Labour Party, and in that capacity wrote many memoranda and pamphlets, particularly on education. For many years he served on the Consultative Committee of the Board of Education, and he was a member of the Committee that produced the Hadow Report in 1926. Over the years he also wrote many leading articles on education for *The Manchester Guardian*. He stood three times for Parliament.

In 1931 he refused a peerage. For a short period from 1940 he served as Labour adviser in the British Embassy at Washington, and in that capacity he put powerful presentations of the British case to the American public.

Bishop Charles Gore introduced him to the tradition of Christian social and Christian socialist thought which in the immediate past went back through men like Bishop Westcott to F. D. Maurice. Westcott had played a large part in the Christian Social Union (founded in 1889, the year of the great dock strike) and had said to the Church Congress of 1890 that 'wage labour, though it appears to be an inevitable step in the evolution of society, is as little fitted to represent finally or adequately the connexion of man with man in the production of wealth as in earlier times slavery or serfdom'.

Over the years Tawney was involved in a number of church commitments. In 1918 he was a member of the Archbishop's Committee on Christianity and Industrial Problems (a fruit of the largely abortive National Mission of Repentance and Hope of 1916). Its report, said a disgruntled Hensley Henson, was dominated by 'Messrs Lansbury and Tawney and their episcopal shadows', an exaggeration which revealed something of the resistances with which Tawney felt himself confronted in the Church of England.[4]

Tawney was involved in the COPEC conference at Birmingham in 1924 (Conference on Christian Politics, Economics and Citizenship). The report of Section IX on 'Industry and Property', of which he was a member, follows the general line of his *The Acquisitive Society*, which had appeared in 1921. He was also at the Jerusalem conference of the International Missionary Council in 1928, and was mainly responsible for drafting the report on industrial conditions in the Mission Field (as it was then called). This was one of the milestones in the development of the Ecumenical Movement. Another was the Oxford Conference on 'Church, Community and State' in 1937. By this time Tawney was becoming impatient with the Churches, which he thought prevaricated on the central issue of the unchristian nature of capitalism. In a memorandum prepared in advance for the Oxford Conference he wrote of the distinctively Christian contribution: 'I have almost ceased to expect that that contribution will come from men or institutions described as Christian.' He removed this sentence when the paper was finally published in *The Attack* in 1953. At the Oxford Conference I was asking him after one session how things had gone in his section, and he replied with a mixture of exasperation and humour that there had been an interminable statement from a Welsh Archdeacon on the Trinity and the coalmines, but as he appeared to want them nationalized it came out all right in the end.

Tawney's books are not very numerous. Mr A. J. P. Taylor has remarked that the unwritten works of Tawney are among 'the lost masterpieces of the twentieth century'. His historical books from the first, *The Agrarian Problem in the Sixteenth Century* in 1912, remain key ones for the student of economic history, as are the selections of documents in English economic history, which he produced with A. E. Bland and P. A. Brown in 1914, and in Tudor economic history which he edited with Eileen Power ten years later.[5] The long projected economic history of the Commonwealth period was never written. Controversy rages as to whether he was right about what was happening to the economic status of the gentry in the first half of the seventeenth century, but that is not our concern now. The last of his historical writings was *Business and Politics under James I*, which appeared in 1958 when he was 78, and was a study of Lionel Cranfield, Earl of Middlesex, as a merchant and a minister of the Crown. It is a pity that he never wrote other than occasional pieces on nineteenth-century England, but as his published historical work is so largely concerned with Tudor and Stuart times it was fitting that the *Festschrift* in honour of his eightieth birthday, edited by F. J. Fisher, his successor in the Chair of Economic History at London University, should be *Essays in the Economic and Social History of Tudor and Stuart England*, covering what he calls 'Tawney's century', roughly 1540–1640.

Among a wider public it is the influence of his two 'tracts for the times', *The Acquisitive Society* and *Equality*, which has been so remarkable. Behind them lies the Christian social teaching whose decay is investigated in *Religion and the Rise of Capitalism*. The influence of this book with both an academic and a wider public has been such that Tawney is in danger of being thought of as *homo unius libri*. Associated with this are his Preface to *Wilson's Discourse upon Usury* (1925) and his introduction to Talcott Parsons's English edition of Weber's *The Protestant Ethic and the Spirit of Capitalism* (1930), Beyond the books already mentioned there are only two volumes of collected essays, *The Attack* (1953) and *The Radical Tradition* (published posthumously in 1964, for Tawney had died in 1962), and *Land and Labour in China* (1932). This last was the product of a visit to China under League of Nations auspices in 1930, and the first critical analysis of the Chinese land problem ever attempted.

A good deal of the influence of his books is due to their style. The closely packed sentences and paragraphs, sparkling with epigrams, weave a texture which is unmistakable. They can scarcely be matched for sustained irony. The mind is teased by what are popularly known as wisecracks, over which it cannot linger because the narrative carries it along. Such a style is the despair of the note taker. He can only give up and listen. I once heard him open a public lecture on 'Marx as an Historian' with the sentence, 'The fate of all great minds is dilution by the world and petrifaction by the elect; Marx more than most.' Before we had recovered from that we were already well launched. Some of these aphorisms occur more than once; that particular one is used in a modified form in a review of *Christianity and the Social Revolution* (reprinted in *The Attack*).

Anyone who visited Tawney in Mecklenburg Square in Bloomsbury (where he and his wife made their home from the 1920s – he had married Jeannette Beveridge, Lord Beveridge's sister, in 1909) – would have wondered how anything ever got written. Books and papers lay everywhere. One deduced there was a table in the centre under piles of them. Presiding over the chaos would be Tawney, smoking a vile herbal tobacco and lighting his pipe with endless matches. My chief picture of him, however, is lecturing in an old pair of flannel trousers and brown jacket and continually pushing his spectacles on to his forehead as he talked. He never seemed to wear any other clothes, even on formal occasions. It is said that he wore his sergeant's tunic for years after the war until it disintegrated and that this brown jacket, designed rather like it, was its successor.

My memory of him is of a profoundly courteous, generous and humble man. It came out in the Professor who never directly or indirectly referred to his own books. It came out in the way he gave a generous welcome to, and took time and trouble over, the most immature student who came his way. He had an unselfconscious goodness which taught me much about the graces of a Christian character. It is no surprise to find Hugh Gaitskell saying, at the memorial service for him, 'Looking back quite objectively, I think he was the best man I have ever known. The quality of his goodness was such that it never embarrassed you.' A friend once said to William Temple, 'What we need are more men like Tawney', to which Temple replied, 'There are no men like Tawney.'

II *Calvinism and Capitalism*

We turn first to *Religion and the Rise of Capitalism* because there is to be found the source of the ideas in his contemporary tracts. It originated as the first series of Scott Holland Memorial Lectures in 1922, 'Religious Thought on Social Questions in the Sixteenth and Seventeenth Centuries', and was published under the new title in 1926. It remains the most noteworthy contribution to a debate which has raged ever since Max Weber's essay *Die Protestantische Ethik und der Geist des Kapitalismus* appeared in 1905. Once of the earliest essays in the sociology of religion, it has been the occasion of more controversy than any other. Troeltsch's massive work *The Social Teaching of the Christian Churches* (1911 in Germany; English translation in 1931) had broadly accepted Weber's thesis. Tawney, however, is cautious. He explores the process of secularization as it bore on economic life, in the way indicated by a paragraph from pp. 26f., which will also serve as an instance of his style.

There is a moral and religious, as well as a material, environment, which sets its stamp upon the individual, even when he is least conscious of it. And the effect of changes in this environment is not less profound. The economic categories of modern society, such as property, freedom of contract and competition, are as much part of its intellectual furniture as its political conceptions, and together with religion, have probably been the most potent force in giving it its character. Between the conception of society as a community of unequal classes with varying functions, organized for a common end, and that which regards it as a mechanism adjusting itself through the play of economic motives to the supply of economic needs; between the idea that a man must not take advantage of his neighbour's necessity, and the doctrine that 'man's self-love is God's providence'; between the attitude which appeals to religious standards to repress economic appetites, and that which regards expediency as the final criterion – there is a chasm which no theory of the permanence and ubiquity of economic interests can bridge, and which deserves at least to be explored. To examine how the latter grew out of the former; to trace the changes from a view of economic activity which regarded it as one among other kinds of moral conduct, to the view of it as dependent upon impersonal and almost automatic forces; to observe the struggle of individualism in the face of restrictions imposed in the name of religion by the Church and of public policy by the State, first denounced, then palliated, then triumphantly justified in the name of economic liberty; to watch how ecclesiastical authority strives to maintain its hold upon the spheres it had claimed and finally abdicates them – to do this is not to indulge in vain curiosity, but to stand at the sources of rivulets which are now a flood.

In this process of secularization Tawney finds three elements: (1) Instead of having a supernatural sanction, human affairs are thought to operate in self-contained departments each with a law of its own. (ii) Instead of society being thought of as an ordered hierarchy it is viewed individualistically and mechanistically. (iii) Instead of generally accepted moral standards based on natural law, with the church as the final authority and in the last resort exercising a discipline in economic matters, the argument is entirely in terms of moral expediency. The result is 'that the attainment of material riches is the supreme object of human endeavour and the final criterion of human success'. Tawney adds: 'Compromise is as impossible between the Church of Christ and the idolatry of wealth, which is the practical religion of capitalist societies, as it was between the Church and the State idolatry of the Roman Empire' (p. 280).

Tawney found the source of the change in the social and economic ferment at the time of the Reformation, and in a series of brilliant passages he sketched the reactions of different Christian groups to it. There was Luther, the romantic conservative, stricter in his views than the Schoolman but removing the sanctions which in theory they operated. There was Calvin, the urban thinker, who realized that interest is no more than an equivalent of rent and that therefore what the Bible and the Fathers said about usury was no longer relevant, and who thus provided a theological foundation for the basic economic virtues, but accompanied it with the most rigorous economic discipline that any church has ever tried to impose. There was the Church of England, characteristically maintaining a traditional and conservative position. And later there were the Puritans in whom, not without a struggle, the economic virtues of Calvin's double approach overcame the disciplines he advocated.

Although we are not primarily concerned with the continuing controversy on the relation of Calvinism to capitalism, a slight digression on it may be useful. It is often called the Weber–Tawney thesis, but this is misleading. Tawney in his Introduction to Parsons' translation of Weber, and in 1937 in the important Preface to the Pelican edition of *Religion and the Rise of Capitalism*, makes important reservations which are often ignored. He points out (i) that Weber only claimed to be carrying out a preliminary investigation into the social influence of different religions and not to be formulating a general theory; (ii) that most of his examples came from the English Puritans of the later seventeenth century; (iii) that there was a general shift of religious thought on economic questions – both Catholic and Protestant – and that Calvinism was not as unique as Weber made out.[6] But he adheres to the link between later Calvinism and the capitalist virtues, stressing that the most significant point is the way mounting economic momentum in the century after Calvin led to the triumph of one half of his economic policy over the other. He also points out that contemporaries were well aware of this connection. It was not first pointed out by Weber.

Subsequent discussion has been powerfully influenced by whether capitalism is unpopular (as in the 1930s), when adherents of various Christian confessions were reluctant for them to be associated with its origins, or whether it is more popular (as in the welfare capitalism of today), when they are inclined to be pleased if they were. It has also been swayed by those whose philosophies demanded either a 'materialist' or a 'spiritual' interpretation of history.

On the whole the support for the capitalist virtues by later Calvinism has been endorsed.[7] An exception is Kurt Samuelsson's *Religion and Economic Action* (published in Sweden in 1957 and in England in 1961) which argues that the Calvinist–Puritan teaching was a quite small element, which has been violently exaggerated, in a broad and general phenomenon. The whole discussion is beside the point; there is no clear correlation of any significance between economic development and changes in religious belief. He demolishes a naïve interpretation of Weber, and some of Weber's evidence, but is prone to overstate the contrary case without paying enough attention to Tawney's mediating position. They both agree in their interpretation of Baxter, the chief witness for later Puritanism, that he preaches *both* diligence and thrift *and* contentment and restraint; he has in mind mainly the small trader carrying on his business for the general good with no special aspirations to develop it. Tawney holds that other strains in Puritanism – notably the idea of the calling – swamped Baxter's restraints. Samuelsson disputes this. Tawney appears to have the better of it; the collapse of the traditional Christian teaching in Protestantism after Baxter supports his more modest thesis, though he deals with it only briefly.

Returning from our digression, the main question for us in Tawney's book arises from his trenchant remark, 'The social teaching of the Church had ceased to count because the Church itself had ceased to think' (p. 188). This is not quite true because Calvinism did crystallize its ethic round the new commercial society, and in a more confused way Catholic moral theologians were to follow. The point is that it did not think fast or far enough. It clung too long to a theory and a control which it could no longer enforce because it was blind to the empirical evidence of what was happening. Its understanding of natural law prevented it from arriving at a proper understanding of the autonomy of the secular. It did not see what was right in the new autonomous disciplines. It failed to provide a theological basis which would both do justice to them and at the same time expose their pretensions.[8] Tawney does not bring this out. He does not see it quite like this, and the fact that he does not leads him to some over-simplified judgments on the twentieth century, as we shall see. But he rightly points out that in an age of impersonal finance, world markets and capitalist organizations, the church tried to moralize economic relations by treating every transaction as a law of personal conduct. This is to say that in its individualism it failed to comprehend the new structures of economic life and the power relations that went with them. There is no doubt about the consequences. Traditional Christian thought became increasingly irrelevant, and in the end capitulated uncritically to the *laissez-faire* view of the state and the economic order. This was to be the starting-point of Tawney's two tracts for the times.

III *The Acquisitive Society*

There has been only one modern systematic Christian discussion in Britain of property, the symposium *Property: its duties and rights*, edited by Charles Gore in 1913. The only other one is an American symposium, *Christianity and Property*, edited by Joseph Fletcher in 1948. There has not been a British edition of this. The ideas in Gore's symposium are in the background of Tawney's *The Acquisitive Society* (1921).[9] After the first world war there was, as now, talk of increased productivity. Tawney's starting-point is that social institutions express moral values, and that disorder in these is more basic than issues of poverty and productivity. The theme of the book is the contrast between an acquisitive and a functional society.

In the acquisitive society a mechanistic *laissez-faire* reigns. Social institutions are not subject to moral criteria. There is no sense of common purpose. What is human and lovable (indeed what is Christian in Christianity) has largely disappeared. Property rights are absolute, without reference to function or service. (Mining royalties and ground rents are particularly noxious.) Limited liability, since the Act of 1855, has led to passive ownership through the separation of management from ownership, and thus to power without responsibility. In short, things no longer serve persons. The traditional Christian defence of property is quite inapplicable to modern industrial society. The attack on the privileges of pre-industrial England was justified, but it has had an unexpected and unfortunate result in industrial capitalist society.

By contrast a functional society enshrines certain simple and unchanging principles, which nevertheless are compatible with more than one type of social organization. These principles are three: (i) Rights depend upon service performed. (ii) The producer must be directly related to the consumer, so that his responsibility is obvious and not indirect through the shareholders. (iii) Authority must be responsible, and conversely, an obligation to service must be laid upon a sense of professional standards in those who supply it. Effectiveness (by which Tawney appears to mean efficiency) is to be achieved by getting rid of functionless property, of hire and fire methods, and by mobilizing the latent professional pride of the worker. Somewhat vaguely it is said that he will share with consumers in governing industry.

Nearly all the explicitly Christian references are in the last chapter. It includes a justifiable attack on the abandonment of the corporate Christian social tradition and the concentration on a purely personal morality, and a more dubious call to the church to discipline its members, to get back from its present privileged position to the situation that prevailed before AD 313, and then to aim 'to make a new kind, and a Christian kind, of civilization'.[10]

Here Tawney has been misled by his theological mentor,

Charles Gore. In his exposition of *The Sermon on the Mount*, first published in 1896 and reprinted many times, Gore makes the unexceptionable point that the Sermon is the moral law of a new kingdom. But he goes on to show that he understands this in a way very different from theologians today by saying that it is 'a law which, recognized and accepted by the individual conscience, is to be applied in order to establish a new social order'.[11] What is missed out is the eschatological background of the Sermon, derived from the meaning of the term 'kingdom of God' and Jesus' relation to it. Just as, in A. N. Whitehead's words, Christianity is a religion always in search of a metaphysic, so it is always in search of a new social order (though the church has often forgotten it). But the idea that there is *a* new social order, and some Christian law or principle which can be simply realized in it through the influence of the church, is quite alien to the teaching of Jesus. In Tawney's thought there is the idea that there is such an order, and that the abolition of functionless private property is the main item in establishing it. There are several empirical forms it could take, there are a number of difficulties to be surmounted, but the basic change required by Christian principles would have been made.

Tawney's two societies would better be regarded, like St Augustine's two cities, as representing two perennial tensions in human life as long as mankind is *in via*, rather than as simple empirical possibilities. His own view has led to an element of utopianism in his thought. He denies that there is a conflict of interest in man himself between his role as a producer and his role as a consumer, or in society between the producers of particular goods and services and consumers of them.[12] In a revealing passage he assumes that 'poor human nature' is waiting to do simple duties and honest work if only the systems which men 'too ingenious to have imagination or moral insight' invent to bully it into efficient work will let it.[13] He tends to overplay the element of professionalism in the professions (as anyone who reflects on the recent behaviour of the medical profession in Britain, Belgium and the United States will notice), even though in another context he says that there is nothing 'more sordid in the occupations which are called trades than there is in the occupations which are called professions. Compared with that of a barrister, the work of building a house, or extracting coal, or manufacturing cotton piece-goods, is a school of morals.'[14]

Tawney does not allow enough for the role of conflict between different groups in society. There will always be clashes of opinion and struggles for power, simply because man's reason is not a neutral element of his make-up but is always to some extent the servant of his interests; and interests differ. Those who give orders and those who receive them see things differently.[15] A man may function in both roles in different parts of his life, just as he has different interests as a producer of one thing and a consumer in general[16] or as a national of one state and as a member of the whole human race. The job of social policy is to ensure that the inevitable group conflicts of interest are creative and not disruptive. The job of Christianity is to mitigate the furies of self-righteousness into which each side can so easily fall, not by pretending there is no conflict or that there is nothing to choose between either side of it, but by witnessing to a righteousness which is greater than our causes. This is to say that we need a theology of power. To run away from power is to be irresponsible. Certainly we need to be alive to its abuses, but also to its potentialities for maximizing divergent interests as a condition of creativeness in the social order.[17] The trouble with the utopian left is that it has tended to ignore the inevitability of social conflict and to leave it to the Marxists to stress it, prior to the classless utopia, or to Tories to stress it as a permanent condition of life since there will be no utopia.

Tawney is quite right, though, in maintaining that the Christian tradition on private property needs complete rethinking in terms of industrial capitalism, and in pointing out that whatever justification there is for it in that tradition requires the widest possible distribution of it, and is quite incompatible with present-day inequalities. That was to be the theme of his second tract.

Tawney was further misled by Bishop Gore on the question of church discipline. In *The Social Doctrine of the Sermon on the*

Mount in 1904 Gore had argued that no one could deny that the church was intended by Christ to be 'a society with a common moral law, which was to be constantly and authoritatively re-applied by way of legislation in general principle, and applied by way of discipline to individuals, in admitting them or refusing to admit them into the Christian Society, retaining or refusing to retain them in membership'.[18] What Gore thought no one could deny it would be very hard to find a New Testament scholar maintaining today as a right understanding of Jesus' ethical teaching. There is indeed a problem in elaborating a distinctively Christian way of life in the mixed societies in which Christians live, and particularly in Western civilization, the only one in which Christian beliefs have moulded the structures of life far beyond believing Christians. Doubtless also some church discipline is necessary. There must be limits beyond which a Christian cannot go without reprimand (though in practice the issue tends to be avoided because the offender cuts himself off from the church, a solution which is not the best for either side). There is the further problem of finding the will of God for the structures of life, or Orders of Creation, in which he places Christians willy-nilly with men of all beliefs and none, and which cannot depend on the people in the structures being committed Christians. (A country like Eire is rare in the history of the church.) But none of these questions can be solved by treating the Sermon on the Mount as the source of legislation of general principles.

It follows that the Christian civilization which Tawney mentions cannot be based on the simple enactment of some Christian principle. Judged by the radical ethic of Jesus, no civilization has ever been Christian or ever will be. True, God sets no limits to the possibilities of achieving such qualities as justice, but neither are there limits to the possibilities of injustice. The Christian shares in the task of furthering the one and avoiding the other. He should be alert to the corruptions which lie in wait for and feed on achievements, for to imagine that particular embodiments of justice are more than partial is to fall a prey to fanaticism, and to give too great a Christian sanction to what is imperfect. This is precisely the error which Tawney traced in the medieval Christian social tradition without quite putting his finger on the source of it.

A Christian civilization, therefore, is one which allows and expects a word of God which judges its partial achievements. It is one which knows how unchristian, in an ethical sense, it is but which is not paralysed by this. It draws upon the divine resources of renewal, and answers the divine call to realize the maximum possibilities at the given moment.

The church may well be in some sense the conscience of such a civilization, provided that it remembers that judgment begins with the household of God (1 Peter 4.17). But it is in a much more ambiguous position than the picture of Gore and Tawney allows. When there comes a challenge in the name of justice, equality or love (we shall consider the relation of these to one another in a moment), the church is inevitably part of the problem and not merely the cure. The conflicts of interest are represented in its own membership, the struggle to see things straight is in its own soul. Its temptation is to take a safe, neutral position above the dispute. This in fact backs the *status quo*. It is unrealistic to expect it to accept change in the power structures all at once, in a single consensus or by a single exercise of discipline. In any case challengers need sifting. Not every claim to improve the social order can be sustained. The church should tolerate the advance guard of Christians committed to change in the structures of power, and be alert to accept the evidence of a valid challenge if they prove their case. This may sound a commonplace, but it is far from the way the church has usually behaved. It has tended to tag along in the rear, slowly adjusting itself to changes after they have taken place, and rarely guiding them. It is this story on the economic front that Tawney has traced. Perhaps it is in race relations that the challenge comes clearest today. What will the verdict be?

IV *Equality*

In 1961 the SCM Press published for the Christian Frontier

Council the report of an enquiry, *Equality and Excellence*, written by Daniel Jenkins. He refers to Tawney's *Equality* as 'one of the most effective publications in the whole of British history',[19] and alludes to its magic style, its moral passion, and its cruel statistics. Originating as the Halley Stewart Lectures in 1929, it was published in 1931, re-issued with a new preface and final chapter in 1938, issued again, with an epilogue, in 1950; and has just been issued yet again, with an introductory chapter by Professor Richard Titmuss.

Tawney improves upon his account in *The Acquisitive Society* of the attack on the legal privileges of the old régime. It was intended to produce a society of property owners, giving equal concern to equal incomes, and ensuring that the inequalities were due to personal qualities and not to arbitrary factors. But industrialism has produced a quite different result. We need to go on from political democracy and legal freedom to the removal of special economic privileges and irresponsible economic power. Why? So that there may be a spirit of freedom and common humanity in social relationships, and that differences of character and intelligence do not lead to great economic and social differences. 'Clever men, it has been remarked, are impressed by their difference from their fellows; wise men are conscious of their resemblance to them' (p. 83). He pleads for a Christian humanism (Maritain would call it a *humanisme integrale*), the opposite of which is a materialism which tolerates vulgar differences of class and income and is in fact a 'tranquil *in*humanity' (pp. 84f.). The key positions in the economic system must be taken out of private hands; a decisive break with capitalism is called for because it treats men as less than men and makes riches a God. It canonizes the *appetitus divitiarum infinitus*. The fundamental dogma of Socialism is the dignity of man (p. 197). The Labour Party must fight not for the claims of particular groups of wage-earners in the present system but for a socialist commonwealth (p. 208). The traditional division of function between labour and management must come to an end, for the problems concern both (p. 177). Tawney does not develop this last point even as far as he had in his previous tract.

In one section Tawney considers and dismisses the conservative case that culture is only possible on the basis of inequality (pp. 81ff.). This is the point which *Equality and Excellence* takes up with some vigour. It stresses the moral obligation of those who are capable of excellence in any sphere to pursue it *for the common good*, and not relapse into a cosy domesticity. Indeed, to elicit the best from one's neighbour one needs to give the best of oneself. Here, however, another problem looms up. How are the less gifted to live with their lack in a society from which the more arbitrary privileges of wealth have been removed and they can no longer hide behind the unfairness of the system? Michael Young's 'meritocracy', a term coined in 1959,[20] is no fanciful menace. Yet it is no excuse for not making a bigger attack on present inequalities, though it is well to realize that the solution of one problem reveals another. Tawney more than once insists that equality is not advocated merely in order that everyone shall be free to 'get on' according to his abilities, but that they should be free to share in 'the good life' in solidarity with their fellows.[21] We cannot regard men as brothers unless in some sense we share their lives.

Tawney is surely right that the Christian faith should have a major contribution to make at this point. There are strong Christian grounds for favouring equality, as soon as it is realized that the Christian belief in the significance of persons cannot be confined to a purely ecclesiastical sphere. It can, however, be held by others, though less powerfully, without the Christian sanction. It was held by the Stoics. Then there is the Utilitarian principle 'everybody to count as one and nobody for more than one'. *Equality and Excellence* quotes a powerful statement of it by Walter Lippmann.

There you are, sir, and there is your neighbour. You are better born than he, you are richer, or you are stronger, you are handsomer, nay you are better, wiser, kinder, more likeable; you have given more to your fellowmen and taken less than he. By any and every test of intelligence, or virtue, or usefulness, you are demonstrably a better man than he, and yet – absurd as it sounds – these differences do not matter, for the best part of him is untouchable and incomparable and unique and universal. Either you feel this or you do not; when you do not feel it, the superiorities that the world acknowledges seem like mountainous waves at sea; when you do feel it they are slight and impermanent ripples upon a vast ocean.[22]

There is a devastating passage in *Equality* (pp. 33 ff.) about some who do not feel this. And there are Christians today who, like Walter James, point out approvingly that Christianity has always favoured an unequal and hierarchical society and that this will put it in a good position to help us to live with the inequalities that a technological age will necessarily bring.[23] But equality can no more be dismissed than can justice. The need to pursue justice arises whenever there is more than one neighbour whose claims have to be considered. Equality is needed as a criterion to test the partial achievements of justice, as anyone who has tried to resolve childish disputes in a family cannot fail to know. It stands in an intermediate position between love and justice. Liberal Christians of the more sentimental type have tended to despise it as compared with love, and more orthodox Christians, realizing that it can never (any more than justice) be perfectly attained, have tended to relegate it to a purely transcendent sphere. It then becomes irrelevant to this world, where private charity alone is left to mitigate the wrongs of the social order. It is true that equality cannot be pursued without regard to efficiency and freedom; it may be granted that special functions and special diligence may need special rewards and privileges, that, in Orwell's inspired slogan, 'All are equal but some are more equal than others';[24] but it remains that those who obtain these differentials will be tempted to claim more than is necessary to get the function discharged for which they are the reward, and that the burden of proof for the Christian must always lie with the inequalities. Tawney's challenge to the conventional Christian position must be accepted.

Equality and Excellence agrees that Tawney's demand for equality must still be pursued in our more prosperous and less unjust society. Of the extent of the economic inequalities in British society there are indeed plenty of cruel details in Tawney's pages, and Titmuss's introduction to the latest edition shows how much still remains. This is particularly true of property as distinct from income. Precisely accurate figures are hard to achieve but reasonably accurate ones show that in 1936 55% of private property in this country was owned by 1% of the population, in 1947 50% and in 1956 42% This year it is possible that 50% of it is owned by 2%, and even this change may mean no more than gifts by tax-conscious parents to their children, leaving the position as between families unchanged. There is in fact a built-in tendency to inequality in our economic system, to capital gains for those who already possess capital.[25] And because the tax rates are so penal and the loopholes so great, death duties have been transformed into what has been called an 'accountant's joke' and 'a tax on those ignorant of the law or suspicious of their families'.[26] The capital gains tax may deal with one aspect of inequality of incomes, but the great weight of inherited inequality of property can only be dealt with by (i) preventing the evasion of death duties by giving one's property when alive to one's family, (ii) removing the inscrutable provision that inherited agricultural land is only taxed at about half rates, and (iii) relating the tax payable to the amount inherited, thus inducing rich people to spread their wealth more evenly.

It is worth pointing out that Lord Randolph Churchill prepared something similar to these suggestions for the budget he never introduced in 1886. Radicals in general have long been shocked by these inequalities of property and the complacency, inefficiency and injustice to which they give rise Radicals are against privilege. Conservatives, too, find *some* place for equality in their thought. Socialists make it their chief criterion. Some of our present inequalities are clearly indefensible on any Christian doctrine of property Tawney's protest remains valid. A just society will have a built-in tendency towards equality.

In no sphere do these inequalities have a more distorting effect than in education, and in none other than that of children does it appear more unjust that they should do. This particularly aroused Tawney's wrath. As the discussions raging in this country at the moment show, the Education Act of 1944 has made only a small dint in the legacy of parsimony and injustice castigated by him, whilst the privileged private sector flourishes like the psalmist's green bay tree, and there is little sign of the sequel, 'I went by, and lo, he was gone: I sought him, but his place could no where be found' (Ps. 37.37).

V *The Later Tawney*

The papers printed in *The Attack* and *The Radical Tradition* are either revisions of ones published at various times since 1916, or a straight reprint of more recent ones. In several, Tawney takes up again the moral basis of the condemnation of capitalism and advocacy of socialism against the background of the Christian social tradition. Concern for the person and for the individual conscience is repeatedly stressed as the basis of his democratic socialism. 'Capitalism corrupts human relations by permitting the use of man by man for pecuniary gain.'[27] The motives of capitalism are entirely wrong and anti-Christian; they appeal to human greed and self-interest and hence involve human beings in wrong relations with one another.[28] Capitalism should be condemned outright by the church.

There is an element of utopianism here which we shall consider shortly. But if Tawney was to some extent a utopian he was a 'hard' one (as the Marxist is in his different way), and not a 'soft' one like many liberals. History, he says, is not so much a sober, sedate and respectable affair as tragic, sublime and disreputable.[29] The heart of his proposals came to be that 'the key points and strategic positions of the economic system shall be removed from the sphere of private interests and held by public bodies'.[30] Granted this change, Tawney makes many allowances for the recalcitrance of human nature and the limitations of political possibilities. Men may have to be persuaded to be free.[31] Planning should be confined to the essentials; it is a serviceable drudge and not a panacea. Values must be allied with interests if they are to become a power in everyday life, and the interests impose their own limitations.[32] The revised version of his Oxford Conference paper contains some drastic criticisms of totalitarianism missing from the original. In this paper he also says that the devil of materialism can easily sway a more egalitarian society. 'If the condition of something approaching full employment were established, both the power and the responsibility of Organised Labour would be greatly increased. It might abuse the former and ignore the latter.'[33] A Trade Union can practise corporate selfishness. In a war against the idolatries of riches and power no final victories are won, and Christians are not likely to be short in the future of lessons to preach or objectives to attack. That does not absolve them from relating themselves to the problems not of twenty years' time, but of today.[34]

Twelve of those twenty years have now passed. It is clear that Tawney was aware of these new issues when using the device of the hypothetical possibility in writing of them. The question remains whether he should have dealt with them without considerable modifications in the proportions of his thought, and in his assumptions.

Consider his moral condemnation of capitalism. Traditionally socialism was concerned with 'the nationalization of the means of production, distribution and exchange'. Thirty years ago this had added force because of the appalling failure of capitalism. There were six million unemployed in Germany, nearly three million in this country. Statesmen wrung their hands but considered it an act of God about which men could do little except ambulance work while they waited for natural forces of recovery to take effect. The social fabric could not stand such stresses. They were the immediate occasion of Hitler's seizure of power and hence a main cause of the second world war. It looked as if the Marxist analysis of capitalism as doomed to crack of its own contradictions was right. But it proved wrong. Economic techniques are now much more sophisticated (here the contribution of J. M. Keynes has been of great importance), and if statesmen have the will they can avoid cyclical depressions and mass unemployment. Of course they may not have the will. They may be recalcitrant, as they are at the moment in the financing of international trade. But the terms of the discussion are now altered in a vital respect from the 1930s.

There are other respects in which it has altered. Welfare capitalism has produced not only a more stable society but also a more affluent and more just one. Moreover, further evidence from the Soviet Union has shown the dangers of economic and political power being in the hands of the same group. Again the belief in progress, a belief not cogently argued out but part of the air breathed by many Socialists, a belief that held that a morally better society is inevitably on the way and that it will be a socialist commonwealth, such a belief has taken so many hard knocks as to have lost its force. For all these reasons the Labour Party has become much more pragmatic. In spite of Hugh Gaitskell's failure to get Clause 4 removed from its constitution, no one believes that the party intends the nationalization of all the means of production, distribution and exchange. But the fact remains that certain central controls are necessary to its policies. (Indeed they are to those of the other parties; no one would be more shocked than Conservatives at a return to *laissez-faire*.) The controls, as the Labour Party see it, should be over what have been called the 'commanding heights' of the economy. Since this is what Tawney insisted on he might well have called it the key issue of Socialism. But he dismisses this as a 'serviceable drudge',[35] and insists with all the overtones of his Christian faith on the moral basis of Socialism. Was he wise in this? Should politics where possible be at the level of the serviceable drudge, or should it be at a quasi-religious level?

If it be true that capitalism is quite simply anti-Christian, then opposition to it becomes a Christian duty, and for a Christian to defend it is heresy. Tawney's case is that it appeals to greed and self-interest and that is why it is unchristian. Certainly an appeal to greed is unchristian, but is an appeal to self-interest? Allied to this question is another one: whether there is something inherently unchristian in the profit motive.

From such a basic teaching of Jesus as 'Thou shalt love thy neighbour as thyself' we learn on the one hand that Christian *agape* is meant to operate in the run of everyday life and not to be regarded as so sublime as to be irrelevant to it, and on the other hand that it is sufficiently sublime never to be fulfilled in it.

Self-interest has to be allowed for. Indeed it must be harnessed. It is too powerful to be repressed. For one thing, the self is not an isolated unit but a person in community, and the basic social unit, or Order of Creation, is the family. Self-interest involves the family and this sets a certain limit to self-sacrifice. Even the Christian needs the prod that comes from having to work to support himself and his family. Furthermore no other self, or group, is either wise enough or good enough to determine how a particular self can make his best contribution to the world.[36] Society needs to be organized so that the equivalent of the 'unseen hand' makes self-interest and the common good coincide, in order to prevent altruism from being put under a greater strain than it can bear. The defect of *laissez-faire* theory was to assume it would happen without being organized. William Temple puts this very forcibly in his *Christianity and Social Order*: 'A statesman who supposes that a mass of citizens can be governed without appealing to their self-interest is living in a dreamland and is a public menace. The art of Government in fact is the art of so ordering public life that self-interest prompts what justice demands' (p. 42). Tawney read the manuscript of this before it was published. There is no record of what he thought of this point. It is not one he ever explicitly discussed.[37]

Nothing of this, it should be needless to say, is meant to imply that self-interest must be given a *carte blanche*. In the process of being harnessed it must be controlled. It is so powerful that it is all the more easily corrupted by love of riches and the desire for power and glory. It needs a strong government and a strong institutional framework within which it is allowed to operate, and this is a central element in the socialist case.[38]

It follows from this that there is nothing inherently wrong in the 'profit motive'; or in 'the use of man by man as an instrument of pecuniary gain', to repeat Tawney's incautious phrase. Because the 'profit motive' was so idolized in the era of *laissez-faire* its usefulness can easily be forgotten now. Certainly profit, in terms of wages or salaries, is by no means the only incentive in daily work. The desire to be accepted by one's associates or mates and in the community is a strong one; so can be the desire to do a proper job. All must be harnessed. But the appeal to the 'profit motive' cannot be ignored. To contrast the motive of service with the motive of profit as an incentive for work is a mistake. Service is not a simple possibility that can take the place of self-interest. Provided that the market is not distorted by gross inequalities of income; provided that the large and growing area for which corporate provision must be made (because the free market cannot cope with it) is allowed for; that is to say provided that there is effective central direction of the economy, with these major provisos the free market, based on the criteria of profit and loss, is a very convenient way of getting a large section of the economic order carried out efficiently without the intolerable clumsiness and risk of enormous errors which planning everything would involve.[39]

Such an appeal to profit is a wide one. It covers economic incentives for efficiency and pioneering as well as patents, royalties, salary increments, and even preaching fees! But it is necessary to stress once more that the 'profit motive' should not be allowed to exercise the baneful effect it has in the past, and that present inequalities are neither necessary nor right. To quote William Temple again, 'The profit motive is not simply evil, it can have its own right place. But that is not the first place.'[40]

Tawney mentions production and increased productivity only in passing. This is clearly a major problem for us, not least because of the sheer momentum of the economy of the USA which leads the way. We cannot dwell on this now. Suffice it to say that the economically developed countries face the morally difficult task of fostering a high level of production and economic growth, and of learning how to use the surplus over the rising level of what are considered necessities for the benefit of the two-thirds of the world's population which has so far had little share in them. We need a moralist of Tawney's power to shame us in our easy acquiescence in relative plenty. He would continue to scrutinize all inequalities, to insist that those that are necessary are made tolerable by divorcing wealth as far as possible from economic power, and he would echo J. K. Galbraith's well-known contrast between private affluence and public squalor.[41] He would also, I am sure, insist that what we spend at home of our growing national income (whether public bodies or private individuals disposing of their own income) should be spent in ways which further human powers of creativity and enjoyment; this in turn involves a generous and flexible attitude to money. There is a devil here to oppose, for the commercial and industrial pressures of an advanced technological society tend to encourage some of the least attractive characteristics of humanity, such as the desire to show off something new. There is a deep gulf between the Christian faith and the acquisitiveness which hoards on the one hand or engages in conspicuous consumption on the other.

To return to Tawney's moral strictures on capitalism, it appears that it is not so simply anti-Christian as he maintains, nor is socialism so simply an expression of the Christian faith. He makes too direct a connection between that faith and the empirical structures of life. Certainly there are broad considerations derived from the Christian faith which call into question details of the empirical scene and put the onus on their defender (we have seen this to be so in the case of private property), but there are no Christian principles of which a particular economic system can be said to be a simple expression.

The element of utopianism in Tawney's thought can cause confusion. Politics should normally be about penultimate, not ultimate, issues (to borrow terms from Bonhoeffer).[42] It is not *always* so; absolutely basic issues can arise and society be in a feverish state until they are settled. Perhaps the racial situation is in many countries such an issue today. But the body politic, any more than the human body, cannot stand too much fever and, where possible, Christians should help to take the fury out of politics. It then becomes a contest over immediate and middle-range, but not ultimate, issues and between people of conservative and radical tendencies. This is as it should be. There are those who have a marked concern for the wisdom of the past and a proper awareness of the consequences of upsetting established institutions. On the other side there are those who are more concerned with the injustices and inefficiencies of the present order and with the need of reform. Both should be found within the Christian church. In practice they are, but far too many of the former. But to say that socialism is not about immediate issues of public policy but about basic moral or Christian issues is to imply that non-socialists are in important respects immoral or unchristian. It is not an issue which is so clear cut. To take that line is to make politics a substitute for religion.

Unfortunately such an attitude is precisely what suits some Christians and some political enthusiasts. Far too many Christians can only be induced to take public affairs seriously if they can identify a devil with horns and hoofs to oppose. Otherwise they lapse into apathy, which is of course an irresponsible conservatism. They need to learn that is it just the 'nicely calculated less or more' which is of the stuff of politics and where a Christian's civic responsibility under God is to be exercised. The inadequacy of much Christian teaching on this point must be confessed. On the other hand, a lot of the loyal band of party enthusiasts who keep local party organizations going derive their strength for doing so from what amounts to a religious attitude to politics. I mean that there is an element in their zeal which ought only to be given to God. The effect is to give them a good conscience, that they support the right and therefore are themselves all right, on too easy terms, and to enable them too easily to dismiss their opponents as advocates of evil. This has happened to a number in the Labour movement who have been influenced by Tawney. If socialism in his mind followed from principles rooted in the Christian faith, those most keen to acknowledge their debt to him rarely refer to the Christianity but only to the principles. This can be seen very strikingly in Titmuss's introductory chapter to the new edition of *Equality*. He actually refers with regret to the end of utopian thought these days, laments that 'everything becomes a matter of compromise between power groups in society', and assumes that no one cares about politics unless they believe that a radically different order of society is at stake (p. 14).

Those who do not accept or understand the Christian faith

and have been misled by the utopian element in Tawney's thought (without noting his incidental qualifications), often make the mistake of stressing only the dignity of man; they underplay his sinfulness. They allow for his grandeur but not his misery. This is a grievous source either of disillusionment or of fanaticism. It also has the effect of presenting people of conservative disposition with an entirely unnecessary weapon. They are able to scoff at radicals and socialists as impractical idealists who do not understand the realities of human nature. In fact, human sinfulness should be just as much an element in the radical tradition as human dignity, for at least it leads to the conclusion that no man and no group is good enough to exercise power over others unchecked.

The recovery of a greater eschatological note in theology (I refer once more to our present understanding of the kingdom of God and the relation of Jesus' person and teaching to it), has destroyed the utopian element in the socialist case. This was a powerful note of the Christian Socialist movement. Awareness of this in theological circles is undoubtedly the main reason why the Christian Socialist movement has run into the sand. It remains fixed in a theological and political attitude of the past; in neither is it flexible or pragmatic enough. Common ownership remains a panacea, and Christian principles are thought to be all too simply expressed by it. Yet a Christian radicalism is badly needed. This same eschatological note can easily provide Christians with an excuse for escapism; *sub specie aeternitatis* they can see no discernible difference between the different political and economic policies offered, for they are all so far short of the glory of God. In the dark all cats are grey. This leads to the opposite error to utopianism. Surely God's people can be helped to avoid both of them.

We have travelled some way from Tawney in these concluding reflections. I wonder what he would make of them. Would he dazzle me with an aphorism to which I could find no immediate reply? I have a suspicion that he would agree with a good deal because, when meeting the objections of non-socialists or fellow socialists, he shows a lively realism, and almost every

qualification I have made can be found, in passing, somewhere
in his writings. In so far as there is an inadequacy in his thought
it was his theology that misled him; this he never re-examined.
It is notoriously hard to hold the elements of Christian theology
in the right proportions. The dominant tendency in Anglican
theology during Tawney's youth and early manhood is often
called incarnational. It is not a very happy designation because
all Christian theology must surely be incarnational. I have a
great respect for it. But eschatology was its weak point. Theology does matter. Although wisdom neither began nor will end
with us, we are in a position now, through the development of
biblical studies and through the Ecumenical Movement, to
offer a better one.

III

Social Change and Christian Theology

– 6 –

The Scene in Christian Social Ethics[1]

There are several preliminary problems in approaching this theme. First of all, what is to count as social ethics as distinct from individual or personal ethics? There is no clear-cut distinction, and most ethical problems can be approached from either angle. In this essay I shall in fact be more concerned with the economic, industrial and political realms. Within these, however, is attention to be directed to particular issues, or to the future of the theory or method of social ethics? I shall indeed refer to likely future issues, partly to give some concreteness and perspective to the essay; but I shall be more concerned with theoretical issues, if only on the grounds that I earn my living as a moral theologian, and ought to have something to draw upon from that occupation, whereas my analysis of specific problems has no more weight than that of any other thoughtful person who seeks to keep himself well informed by reading current papers and journals. Another question is whether we are to be concerned with the future of social ethics in general – either as to theory or as to particular issues – or with specifically Christian social ethics. Some might think there would be no difference as far as the facts of specific issues are concerned, but 'facts' are always seen in a context of significance. This context may, on occasion, be the same for the Christian as the non-Christian, or it may be different, or it may be partly the same and partly different. The continuing debate on abortion is a good illustration of this. Although there are indeed differences of opinion between Christians and humanists on this issue, there is a general tendency for them to arrive at different conclusions, even if they agree on the facts, because they weight them differently. Hence each tends to think the other is inhuman. Be that as it may, I shall be more concerned with Christian social ethics, for the reason that I am a professional moral theologian and only an amateur moral philosopher. However, social ethics in general cannot be excluded because of the necessity for Christians and non-Christians to live together in the plural society of contemporary Britain.

One more demarcation issue remains. Are we to be concerned with where I think social ethics will go or where it ought to go? As far as particular issues are concerned I shall be more concerned with where it is likely to go, though I am sure value judgments as to where it ought to go will be present, overtly or covertly. But as to the question of theory or method, I am more concerned with where it ought to go, since there seems to me to have been a certain loss of impetus in Christian social ethics since the Oxford Ecumenical Conference on 'Church, Community and State' in 1937 and the death of William Temple in 1944.

Some of the loss of impetus may well arise from the sense of the greater complexity of the issues than in the traumatic decade of the 1930s. This may merely be a personal reaction, and an indication that I am that much older. But I do not think so. We are all much more aware of the complex interlocking of factors, of the 'global village' aspect of life today, and this at a time when Britain has lost a great deal of power and is having obvious difficulty in finding a new role in the world. At any rate I find myself less and less looking for over-all solutions, and more and more sceptical of those who think they possess them. But this does not mean that I have given up taking social ethics seriously, or have any disposition to retire into a private domain of a tacit, and therefore irresponsible because not thought out, conservatism; nor that I do not see the need to pursue utopias in the narrower sense of the word. In his classic work, *Ideology and Utopia*, the English translation of which appeared as long ago as 1936, Karl Mannheim remarks that the complete disappearance of the utopian element in human thought and action would mean the decay of the human will. If man loses his will to shape human history he will lose his ability to understand it.

The listing of these preliminary considerations serves to make even clearer the acute problem of selection that this topic involves There is no escape from this. Whatever is said will reveal yawning gaps, even greater because there are areas where nothing is said; and the whole exercise may perhaps most usefully be seen as a spur to the reader to make his own selection in the light of the inadequacies he sees in this one.

I

It may seem a commonplace to point it out, but the most certain future for social ethics is that it will have to be thought out and lived in a society of increasingly rapid social change. This is propelled by the cumulative force of a succession of dramatic changes in the human situation of sufficient moment to be called revolutions. I can think of six, and they are so familiar as only to require a brief mention. They begin with the break up of medieval civilization. I am sure that it did not seem as stable at the time as it seems now; but relatively to what has followed it was stable. The first of these revolutions was the Reformation. It loosed a radical element in the Judaeo-Christian religion which had been pretty successfully bottled up for centuries, which goes back to the prophetic tradition in the Old Testament and is taken up in the relation of Jesus' life and teaching to the kingdom of God. This radical element soon began to be tamed. In New Testament times we can see this in the Pastoral Epistles. Similarly even the Reformation churches fairly soon settled down into a rigid orthodoxy and settled practice. But not quite. The explosive force of the Reformation was too great. The challenge of *semper reformanda* could not be ignored Now the theme is found in the Roman Catholic Church itself in the documents of Vatican II. Moreover what is asserted of church thought and structures, *ecclesia semper reformanda*, cannot be confined to them; it becomes a source of disturbance in secular life. Calvinism is the best example of this. Its importance can be seen from the fact that the Orthodox churches have never experienced a Reformation. True, their tradition has preserved values that we of the Western churches, Roman Catholic, Anglican and Protestant, need to draw upon; but the lack of this note, *semper reformanda*, is conspicuous in the Orthodox tradition, and nowhere more conspicuous than in its fossilized social ethics. It is this note in the Judaeo-Christian faith which is very hard for a functionalist sociology of religion to accommodate. It always wants to subsume religion under the category of agencies for the reinforcement of established institutions.

The next revolution, in chronological order, was the scientific revolution of the seventeenth century, epitomized by the foundation of the Royal Society in this country in the reign of Charles II with its motto *Nullius in verba*. It is generally agreed that there was a decisive change in European thought and outlook around the years 1680–1715, and it is this which separates us most sharply from that of the Bible. The development of natural science and, as an offshoot, the study of the past by critical methods and the foundation of history as a discipline in the modern sense, has led to a secularization of thought – in particular to a new way of thinking of God's relation to the world – and later to a secularization of institutions. I mean by this the loosening of ecclesiastical control over institutions and customs.

The scientific revolution was quickly followed by one brought about by the application of science, in which this country again led the way. I refer, of course, to the Agricultural and Industrial Revolutions. The effects of these have now spread themselves over the globe with vast social and cultural consequences. It was these which carried the enormous population growth in the industrialized countries. It is the medical services produced by the application of science which has led to the fall in the death rate, and hence the population explosion, in countries which have not yet the technical infrastructure to carry it. Meanwhile the countries of the first Industrial Revolution have embarked on a second one, based not on coal and iron so much as electronics and the search for dramatic new sources of energy.

The fourth revolution has been the anti-Colonial one. A resistance to European hegemony began almost as soon as the social and technical changes in Europe speeded up. It was heralded by the rebellion of the American colonies and the setting up of the United States of America in 1776, and it reached its peak after the end of the second world war in 1945. Little remains of this hegemony now, though much is heard of its economic aftermath in the guise of neo-colonialism.

Next came the proletarian revolution, which can conveniently be dated from the publication of the *Communist Manifesto* in 1848. The extraordinary speed with which the influence of Marxism has spread over the globe since then needs no emphasis from me. It has also shown an ability to escape from a monolithic straightjacket, and to interpret the experience of a vast number of ordinary people, which is most impressive. Indeed, it has been said that Maoism is a kind of Marxism *semper reformanda*. The new leaders of China do not incline to this element in Marxism, but it may well continue to leaven the lump and prevent undue fossilization of what has clearly proved in many respects a most creative change in China.

The last revolution is the anti-white one, and the full force of this is just beginning to be experienced. Its power has so far only been successfully expressed in the ability to raise dramatically the price of oil. For the rest it is epitomized internationally in the uneasy relationships between what are conventionally called the 'north' and the 'south' in the United Nations Conferences on Trade, Aid and Development (UNCTAD); domestically it shows itself in uneasy relationships between white and coloured majorities and minorities. In this country we find, for instance, coloured families who have had the enterprise to settle here living amid some of the least enterprising of our indigenous stock, and we face the crucial test as to whether the children of these families, who have been born and brought up here, will in fact be treated as full citizens on leaving school.

The cumulative effect of these revolutions is the continued erosion of established institutions and authorities. It applies to the family, the school, the church and the state (and to the arts). The certainties by which they operated have been undermined in different ways. Intellectually one has only to mention key names like Marx, Darwin, Freud, Einstein, Crick and Watson (who cracked the genetical code), to be reminded of the immense changes which ideas associated with each of them have brought to accepted ways of thought. In another way, rapid social and technical change has brought a vast increase in mobility. At least it has for the 50% or so of the people of this country who have access to motorized transport. The rest, who are comparatively immobile, have to be content with what the others also get from their TV sets, namely vivid insights into customs and ideas very different from their own; these at least relativize the comparative certainties derived from being locked up in one situation, which has been the position of most people in past ages. This, combined with the increased Gross National Product, produces another revolution, that of rising expectations. We are indeed suffering a relatively slight set-back at the moment; it is unpleasant enough for those who bear the main brunt of it, like unemployed school leavers, but it must not blind us to the longer-term perspective. Our GNP rose 69% in the first twenty-five years of the Queen's reign. (That of West Germany and Japan has risen much more in the same time.) People therefore expect more. They want more consumer durables. They look for more from marriage. The nuclear family is no longer the economic unit it was; it depends more on conviction and consumer satisfaction to hold it together. All this has its effect on established authorities, not least because in many ways youth is most at home in this world. Indeed half the population of the Fourth World is under fifteen. In the industrialized countries the relative affluence of those in work has produced the teenage market, the satisfaction of which proves so profitable. With teenagers being trend setters it is no wonder that authority, in the old sense, is undermined. It is also scandalized. Parental influence is much less direct; schools are more relaxed; universities can no longer adopt a 'take it or leave it' attitude to students. A don has to become a bit of a salesman; he has to make the effort to be interesting to students if he wants to get any work from them. Older ways of exercising authority in industry have had to be drastically modified as 'hire and fire' management has gone. Political parties can no longer count on respect for their established positions. While a minority may be very consciously setting out to 'do their own thing', and the majority may somewhat passively conform to a general ethos, neither is disposed to give much credence to established authorities. This is particularly so as regards the church, which has inherited an imposing structure of buildings representing a dominant 'Christendom' position in the country, which in turn went with at least outward protestations of regard and respect. Not so now. The dwarfing of church towers and spires, which used to dominate the horizon, by other higher buildings, is an outward and visible sign of an inward and spiritual change.

The rapid social change which characterizes our society has had the effect of emphasizing three features of it. First of all it is a plural society, and a secular one. Plural is a much better word to describe it than permissive. It refers to the fact that there is no one generally accepted moral authority, or code, but a variety. That in itself is a relativizing factor. 'Secular' is used to refer both to loss of ecclesiastical control over institutions, and to a general attitude of mind which, if it thinks of God at all, thinks of his relation to man in the world in a different way; and if it does not think of him at all moves in a spectrum from unconcerned agnosticism to an aggressive atheist *secularism* as an explicit ideology.

second feature of our society is that it is future-orientated in a calculating way. It may or may not have a belief in immanent progress (as in Marxism), but it is not willing to leave the future to God, or to chance, if it thinks it can be planned. This is not by any means an easy matter. To draw attention to some of the difficulties is not an incentive to cynicism but to realism. The longer the period ahead that is envisaged the more uncertain the process. Short-term forecasting might be up to fifteen years (which is as long ahead as one thinks if one discounts the future at a rate of 10% p.a.). It is about as long as it might take a major road scheme to proceed from the first idea on a drawing board to coming into use. Yet it is over three times as long as the length of a Parliament, which tends to be the

strongest factor in government strategy. And it is a hazardous
matter to forecast even this short period. Think, for example, of
how many educational calculations have gone wrong between
1962 and 1977. For one thing no demographer knows the rate at
which human beings will decide to reproduce themselves;
government population estimates in this country since the end
of the war have had continually to be revised downwards.
Medium-term forecasts of up to about fifty years are even more
hazardous, and long-term forecasts beyond that still more. It is
unusual to know that, as in the case of the projected Commercial
Fast Breeder Reactor, we are dealing with a highly dangerous
radio-active substance with a half life of 25,000 years. Any use of
a term like 'Futurology', which suggests an entirely spurious
scientific precision in these matters, should be resisted; and
Herman Kahn's prognostications can be read with interest,
but in a sceptical frame of mind.

A further problem for a future-oriented society is the retrieval
and absorption of knowledge. In some branches of sciences it is
probable that four-fifths of what will be relevant knowledge in
the year 2000 is not known at all now. This again brings home
the fact that we live in a world for the young. Most of us have no
new ideas after the age of twenty-five; our reaction to anything
new is to slot it into a familiar mental pigeon-hole and then
assume we have coped with it. Indeed extrapolating from present trends is itself a conservative activity. (This is the element of
truth in the stress, in the 'theologies of hope', on the newness
which God brings about.) From this feature the problem of
adaptability arises. How great an extent and how great a rate of
change can human beings cope with? And how can their increasing desire to participate in decision-making processes be
realized, when these decisions are evidently of increasing complexity, and where it is desirable not to foreclose options for
future generations if we can avoid it? It is noteworthy that electorates often want incompatible things, and are reluctant to give
governments which are subject to defeat at the polls enough
backing to deal with basic policy issues. It is interesting that we
are wanting today both smaller and larger units at the same

time. Nationalism is still a force, even though its scope is less. Local community politics can arouse participation; yet at the same time the number of water authorities has to be drastically reduced if supplies are to be ensured. In the church there is growing dissatisfaction with the parish as an all-purpose unit, and a demand for street and house groups at one end of the scale and Deanery responsibility (and wider than that) at the other.

Perhaps underlying all this is a basic question as to what man's attitude is to be to the new powers at his command and likely to come his way. This, of course, is what Bonhoeffer meant by his talk of 'man come of age',[2] not any suggestion that his moral failures have been overcome. Is he to be brash about these powers? Or timid? Or use them in sober confidence, if possible with reverence and *godly* fear?

The third feature of modern society is that it is evident that we live in one world. So far I have hardly mentioned the global situation. But neither it nor the responsibilities of the relatively wealthy and powerful can be ignored. The 'global village' metaphor is apt. World wars and the technological developments which they have set in train, have brought this about. In food supplies it evidently strikes home, but scarcely less obvious is the fact that air and water currents are no respecters of natural boundaries, neither for that matter is a poisoned earth, on account of the food chain. In this one world we are the first generation which hears the cry of the oppressed from any quarter of the globe. We cannot shut our ears to it. What previous generations did not and could not know they had no responsibility for. We have no such excuse. And this brings out the importance of the question, what common moral understanding is to hold together the mankind which is technologically tied together? If it is only force our future is grim indeed. Harsh necessity may bring some grudging co-operation for fear of what may happen without it. It has been suggested, for instance, that the interests of the workers and employers or managers in a particular industry are completely opposed, but that in the last resort a tolerable *modus vivendi* between them is secured by the fact that they both want the enterprise to go on and not collapse. That is a slightly less grim base than sheer force. But man is capable of something more outgoing than that; his nature and dignity are such that there is something more positive to build on. This brings home the urgency of seeking ways of understanding between men of different faiths and ideologies; in particular it raises for Christians both their attitude to other religions, and the need for Marxist-Christian dialogue. There is much cogency in the prayer which ends with the words 'Save Lord, by love, by prudence and by fear'. God needs to use all the means at his command to weld recalcitrant humanity into tolerable co-existence and co-operation.

II

I turn now to a brief mention of some specific issues in social ethics, to give an element of concreteness to these reflections. But before doing so I must point out that everything depends on the prevention of a nuclear, biological or chemical war. If I pass over this quickly it is because it cannot be treated adequately on this occasion. As to nuclear war, the danger is not so much from the great powers, who are aware of the colossal cost. And the more Russia and China develop economically the more this is likely to be realized. We should assist their development in any way we can. The danger comes rather with the spread of nuclear weapons to smaller powers more confined by parochial horizons, whose actions could engulf us all. I myself think that we need a much more sustained public reflection on the ethics of war, and ought not to give this up as useless or hopeless, but I shall not pursue this further. Another factor which could alter the whole situation, though not so drastically, is the mismanagement of the extremely powerful American economy. After all it was the position of the USA as the world's grain reserve, and its persistent deficits during the Vietnam war, financed by dollar creation, that have been the main factors behind the current inflation. But further consideration of this must be left aside.

Population questions loom in a variety of ways. I leave aside problems of birth and death and refer to coping with those who are vigorously alive. Whilst the logistics of dealing with any significant increase in the population of crowded Britain are considerable, it is as nothing compared with that of feeding, for instance, the population of South-East Asia in ten years' time, not forgetting the transport resources required to get the food there. Then there is the urban explosion. Increased agricultural productivity produces a drift from the land, where less labour is required, to the towns where there are also no jobs, and where the social cohesion and constraints of village life are removed. This is what has made the *favellas* of Latin America, or the city of Calcutta, notorious. How to achieve a tolerable society and avoid an explosion caused by pervasive frustration will call for a high quality of social policies and political skill. Where these situations are compounded with racial strife the dangers are that much worse.

The problems that face our society derive more from our comparative affluence. Can we be content to be part of an affluent sector in a global slum? I should be happier if I thought the Fourth World could exercise some pressure on us, on the grounds that in the political realm it is those who can exercise pressure by their votes or by their economic policies that are likely to be attended to. I do not see the Fourth World being able to exercise that pressure to any great extent, even if it were united to a greater extent than it is. The case of oil seems an exception. Therefore, if fear and prudence may not be very powerful motivators of the wealthy, we are left with love; or if that is too deep a term for what can be expected, we are left with an appeal to a sense of common humanity or the unity of mankind, to which I have already referred.

We are, of course, more preoccupied with our own domestic affairs. We are disconcerted that our welfare capitalist economy, with all its achievements, has failed in so many respects to create the conditions for a good life. Dust, noise, pollution, congestion, bad housing and ugliness are too prominent. In particular there is the question of inequalities of wealth and income.

I assume for the moment that there is a problem of social ethics here, and return to that theme later. The current facts of inequality are coming out through the work of Professor A. B. Atkinson of University College, London, for instance in his book, *The Economics of Inequality*, and the Royal Commission on the Distribution of Income and Wealth, at present sitting. There are considerable difficulties in measuring income and wealth. Roughly it seems that the top 10% in the UK get 25% of the after-tax income. Wealth, however, is much more unevenly distributed. The top 1% own 33% of the wealth; this is as much as is owned by the bottom 50%. If the proportion of wealth were the same as that of income owned, the figure would be only 6·7%. The top 1% represents about 400,000 people (note, for comparison, that there are eight million Old Age Pensioners and over one and a half million unemployed). The top 5% own 55% of the wealth (or 33% if state pensions are counted as wealth). Further, there are serious flaws in the social security system, with its poverty trap, and the forty-four means-tested benefits with their low take-up. In 1956 a married man with two children of school age who earned the national average wage paid no income tax; in 1976 a similar man earning half the national average wage paid tax. In my view this should be corrected by the introduction of a Tax Credit scheme.[3]

The question which lurks in the wings is whether the comparative affluence which sustains our welfare state can continue? Are we reaching an impasse? Should we aim for a zero growth rate, or even a negative one? The 'limits to growth' discussion was launched on the affluent West by the report of that name published in 1972 by the privately sponsored Club of Rome, amid public acclaim and expert criticism. It has been allied with an ecological 'steady-state' theory which is equally suspect. Some Christians have been so carried away by this as to wish to lose man in nature, a monism from which the Judaeo-Christian faith has delivered him. The excitement has died down a little now, chiefly because the whole case was so insecurely founded. It is true that the resources of the earth are finite, but we do not know what the limits are, and have every reason to suppose they are vast. Increased demand for resources produces increased supply. A variety of factors lead to this; new discoveries, the invention of new materials; the use of lower-grade materials; the extraction of hitherto inaccessible materials; and all made possible by further technological development. Our rate of growth is likely to resume before long at a secular trend of about 3% p.a. (A 4% growth would mean a 50% increase in real income in ten years.) As an example, note that suddenly in advanced economies half or more of the employed are engaged in producing or distributing information. Growth in information technology has produced a tenfold reduction in the costs of telecommunication in twenty years, and a thousandfold reduction in computer costs in fifteen years, and it is expected that improvements in performance as against cost will continue throughout this century. The truth in the 'limits to growth' argument lies in the need for careful thought and not brashness in monitoring what is happening to earth, air and water in the process of growth, including the building up and strengthening of appropriate international institutions. The problem is not so much that of a sustainable society as of a just one – nationally and internationally. Adequate trade and monetary arrangements between nations are involved, as is a method of handling conflicts within them on the distribution of income, so that inflation is avoided. Technical possibilities are increasing so fast that there is the possibility that within a century the burden of crippling hunger and toil which has afflicted most of humanity most of the time can be lifted. But since many of the amenities of life which the relatively wealthy appreciate depend on their relative scarcity, and would be eroded if they became available to the mass, some new social attitudes will be needed compared to the major reliance on acquisitiveness which has characterized the development of capitalism. The challenge to the wealthy West will be, what will it do with its affluence?

Certainly as far as this country is concerned, new attitudes to work and to leisure will be called for. At the moment the unemployed youngster is being made to bear the brunt of the adjustment to a society which still operates on a work ethic and which is very ready to talk of scroungers, when there is need for less manufacturing work, there are far fewer unskilled jobs, there is more scope for services, and we are at the beginnings of a situation where leisure can be an acceptable choice instead of seeking a higher standard of living by persistent hard work. But we are confused on these things. We want full employment, a stable price level and free collective bargaining, when the three are incompatible; and we want to raise minimum standards and at the same time maintain traditional and fossilized differentials. It is worth noting that middle-class professional associations with Trade Union functions have been as much involved in this as any of the main Trade Unions. Indeed some of them have been pace-setters.

III

I now wish to refer to five theoretical issues of Christian social ethics which need stressing. The first is the relation betweeen love (*agape*) and justice. Protestant ethics in modern times has had difficulty with this, though classical Lutheranism and Calvinism had their different ways of relating the two, neither entirely satisfactory. The ethical teaching of Jesus appears to be overwhelmingly addressed to personal issues and to be indifferent to collective ones. And the early church was in no position to exercise public responsibility, nor with its apocalyptic outlook was it disposed to do so. In New Testament times standard moral guidance developed only for family relationships, in the shape of the 'household codes'. In so far as these do reveal any tendency, it is a somewhat sinister subordinationist ethic, in which the greater weight is put on the obedience of the less powerful person in the relationship, wife to husband, children to parents, slaves to masters. Questions of justice do not appear. Evangelical Protestantism has also developed an excessively individualist outlook which has led it to suppose that problems of collective ethics can be solved provided we have individually consecrated persons facing them. Thereby half the problem of ethics, acting from the right motive, is faced, but the other half, achieving the right content in action, is evaded. The Archbishops' Call to the Nation in 1975 was one of the latest instances of this. Its two questions, 'What sort of society do we want?' and 'What sort of people do we need to be in order to achieve it?' evade the further questions, 'What sort of structures does that society require?' and 'What steps are needed to move our present structures towards them?' During the period when I marked Christian Ethics papers in the General Ordination Examination I became depressed by the number of candidates who, when faced by a question of social ethics, would ramble on inconsequentially for a while, and then end by saying that Jesus told us to love our neighbours as ourselves, and when we do that the problem will be solved, clearly under the impression that they had thereby vindicated the depth and perspicuity of Christian ethics. Sometimes, however, we do find in modern Protestant ethics a specific discussion of an ethical problem, but with a tendency to move too easily from the Bible to a conclusion about some contemporary social issue without the necessary intermediate steps being examined, or the adequacy of the data of the problem being sufficiently checked. I have recently been dealing with someone who has tried to do this with respect to crime and punishment and prison sentences; he wants to move straight from the teaching of the Old Testament prophets as vindicated in the New Testament, to current English criminological practice. In these cases questions of justice also drop out.

Traditional Roman Catholic moral theology, on the other hand, has developed the Justice Tract very thoroughly, going back through St Thomas Aquinas to Aristotle. But it has had two defects. It has tended to assume that the *status quo* is just and to proceed on that basis, an assumption which has become impossible today. It has also tended so to emphasize justice as a primary Christian requirement that love is in danger of being thought an optional extra, a work of supererogation; we *must* as Christians be just but we *may* be loving. This impression arose because of the apparent absence in the teaching on justice of reference to the New Testament understanding of love. That is why, in recent Moral Theology, books have been written to show that in fact justice is related to *agape* as basic, although it does not appear to be on the surface.

Theoretically we can analyse the concept of justice as follows:

1. Formal justice: has the law been correctly applied?
2. Substantive justice: is the law a just one or not?
3. Retributive justice: (a) commutative (between citizens)
                         (b) corrective (or penal)
4. Distributive justice: (a) recognitive (e.g. *suum cuique*, 'to each his due')
                         (b) attributive

Faced with concepts such as these, some theologians have held that love and justice are opposed, some have said they are identical, and some that they are distinct but related. Brunner and Nygren are modern examples of Christian theologians who have seen *agape* as so essentially personal in character as not to be able to relate directly to issues of social ethics. Fletcher, on the other hand, says that as soon as more than two people are involved, justice is identical with love distributed.[4] This can only be so if love is equated with the content of what is done and not also with the motive for doing it, and if the quantity of love brought about is alone considered and not the manner of its distribution. (This is an old problem in utilitarian or consequentialist ethics.) The third position is to say that love must presuppose justice (charity is no substitute for it), though it transcends it; and on the other hand justice itself implies love to some degree, in that it affirms other as persons and not just as functions.

The most considerable treatment of justice in recent years is that of John Rawls in *A Theory of Justice*, which is likely to be the focus of discussion for some time. It is an attempt to establish, on a rational basis, policy guidelines which reflect a certain view of man, and which are not alien to the Western Christian-humanist tradition. In any case it is important to reflect on Rawl's work from the point of finding a consensus about the common good in a plural society. He is opposed to the consequentialist utilitarian ethic because it is liable to sacrifice the good of some for the sake of maximizing the good over-all, and he tries to establish an alternative basis for society, building upon three suppositions: (i) men are rational and self-interested, but not altruistic nor envious; (ii) men are interested in achieving more rather than less of what satisfies them (what he calls 'the thin theory of the good'); (iii) men are under a veil of ignorance as to the position they will occupy in society, so that rationality requires them to judge from the standpoint of the weakest and poorest in case they should prove to be in that case. On these three assumptions he arrives at two basic social principles, the second being in two parts. They are:

1. There should be an equal right to maximum basic liberties for each (because this is basic to man's self-respect), compatible with a like liberty for all.
2. Inequalities of wealth, power, status and income are only justifiable if
   (a) they are of the greatest benefit to the least advantaged;
   (b) they go with positions which are open to all and under conditions of opportunity for all.

Furthermore, the first principle is prior to the second, and 2(b) is prior to 2(a). Rawls admits that this stress on the priority of liberty presupposes a fair level of wealth, and this is a major qualification, taking the world as a whole, when many lack food and shelter, to say nothing of education. It illustrates the point that the understanding of what is just is related to particular societies and cannot entirely be resolved by abstract argument. I cannot enter in detail into the discussion provoked by Rawls, but Christians can certainly not stand aside from it. To my mind they may well think that Rawls is also too individualistic. People are persons in relations, they are social beings. Why should not their altruism, their *agape* if you like, be called upon as well as their rationality and self-interest? After all, *agape*, as Christians understand it, may well be deepened by Christ but it draws out from man what is already there. And while we have seen that it is naïve to expect to run society on *agape* alone, it is impoverishing to man not to call on it at all. Christians would also, I think, want to give the least advantaged a greater priority.

This raises the second main issue for Christian social ethics, that of equality. There are notorious difficulties here which can only be touched on. Even if we agree that inequalities which are not necessary or justifiable for the common good should be eliminated, it leaves many questions as to what is necessary and justifiable to be resolved. Further it seems clear, though it has often been ignored in practice, that the Christian ethic adds to natural justice a special commitment to the poor. It will not be satisfied with distribution by rights or by merit, it will want to go on to need. But what are needs? Beyond obvious minimum ones there is much scope for argument. And who are the poor? It is not always easy to identify them in our society. Often they are thought to be the unskilled labourers. This is not necessarily the case. They are more likely to be those with large families, the sick, the disabled, the unemployed and the old. On the whole they are likely to lack political power and thus to lose out in power conflicts. Christians should be on the alert to champion them and not be mesmerized by the best organized power groups. It is precisely at this point that Political Theology and Liberation Theology, both of which have come to the fore in the last ten years, but which are only now beginning to touch Britain, have made a forceful challenge, with their mixture both of denunciations of, and calls for, ideologies (and also utopias), and their demonstration of the impossibility in fact of being neutral where the cause of the poor is concerned. Neutrality is tacitly to side against them.

Related to these issues is that of an ethic of power. It is impossible to solve issues of social ethics in terms of a purely personal one. A notable instance of this is that of the Closed Shop, where the proponents of the most clear-cut opposed positions are working within different ethical presuppositions, one personal and the other collective. Once it is seen that a personal ethic cannot resolve collective issues, there is no escape from questions of power, of leadership, of conflict and controversy. Within some basic convictions which hold society together, which have been referred to twice already, there will always be conflicts of power and interest leading to particular and relative solutions or compromises. In handling them, the appreciation of the criteria of prudence and proportion will mitigate the furies of controversy and help the provisional resolution of them to be creative. These considerations are basic to all social interaction. In particular they are part of the life of all those who are drawn into acting in a representative capacity, and involve them in bearing in mind feed-back to those they represent, and how far they can keep ahead of their constituency without being too far ahead.

Christians who find themselves conscientiously opposed to one another in questions of social ethics are helped if their common worship leads them to a proper kind of otherworldliness; one which takes the things of this world seriously. Common worship is both concerned with God through Jesus Christ, who is the same yesterday, today and for ever, and with the particular situation of a particular congregation in a particular place and a particular time. It is here that worship can be unreal, and where the fixities of the 1662 Book of Common Prayer were most inadequate. Today in the era of revised and more flexible services, we are much more free in this respect, but we still do not set the conflicts in the realm of social ethics in the context of God's eternal graciousness in Christ. Too often unreal sentiments which gloss the realities that have to be lived with are all that are uttered.

However, it is not only church worship which needs scrutiny with social ethics in mind, church structures do also. The revival of the sociology of religion as a discipline in the last years has brought this home. Structure and witness go together. As has been noted, we have inherited the structures of a Christendom situation but without the reality of it, and are tempted to a nostalgia for its return. We need to work for their modification more rapidly than increasing economic pressures will in any case bring about. Similarly we need to look more closely at the way the church actually works, as distinct from its ecclesiological theories. It is noteworthy that the Curia is not mentioned in any of the documents of Vatican II, and yet the working out of the new perspectives of that Council depends to a large extent on the nature and composition of the Curia, as has become evident since the Council. Or why are some clergy of the Church of England joining a Trade Union, not in the sense of the 'worker priest' identifying with his workmates, but for self-protection? It is because the combination of factors which decisively influence their conditions of work, including the exercise of *episcope* as pastoral care, does not necessarily ensure that natural justice is observed. A final illustration of a different kind is that a sociological appraisal of church structures would indicate how vital is a reconsideration of the wider responsibilities of the suburban church, the only one where there is a likelihood of relatively large resources of persons and money.

IV

I mention briefly in conclusion the method which seems appropriate for carrying on Christian social ethics. It clearly must proceed on an empirical and not an *a priori* basis. It is the realization of this which had produced the vast changes in Roman Catholic moral theology in the last fifteen years. In particular it is this which has led to the reconstruction of theories of Natural Law as compared with the way the doctrine had come to be used. But if social ethics is to proceed this way it needs information. Information means drawing on the relevant experience of those who are involved in different ways in the issue in question. Some of them may be experts. Yet using experts is not always an easy matter. Experts differ. They may themselves have an axe to grind. Or they may generalize beyond their competence. So the motto has to be, test the expert! Experts may also be attacked by the unorthodox in their field. These are often called cranks. But sometimes the so-called crank is later proved right and the expert wrong. One can't be sure. One can only go by probability. There are inevitable uncertainties.

Progress in social ethics is achieved by varieties of group work: groups of people in the same occupation or in different ones; from the same discipline or interdisciplinary; in one locality or from a whole area; in one congregation or from several; from one confession or ecumenical. There is great scope for variety. But one can say with some assurance that theologians must work with others. It is impossible for theologians to resolve issues of Christian social ethics on their own. The method of co-operative work pioneered by the World Council of Churches from its earliest stages has proved a fruitful and productive example of how to proceed.

In the end questions of social ethics are not resolved in any simple sense. A range of likely options will probably be arrived at, with possibly a general consensus as to the general direction in which to move and the evils to guard against. Some attitudes and actions may come to be practically ruled out, as clearly unchristian, but because of the inevitable uncertainties about the relevant facts of a situation, and of the likely consequences of possible lines of action, there is unlikely to be only one plausible Christian detailed conclusion. Christians equally committed to the same general aims may find themselves adopting different detailed policies.

Is there a Christian social ethic? Not in the sense of detailed conclusions as distinct from a range of considerations which bear upon conclusions. The Christian faith is a reinforcement of motivators to action, not a blue print for it. It reinforces motivation by narratives and parables, especially those concerning Jesus and his mission and message. It calls forth worship, which itself fosters faith, hope and love, in working out the implications in detail. It provides a noble view of the nature and destiny of men, which is not blind to his corruptions, but looks beyond them so that it can hope against hope when human affairs are recalcitrant, and not give up. But none of this avails if Christians are not alert to the actual situations which are the context of social decisions. Here the churches failed for a long time to catch up with the rapid social changes which were referred to at the beginning of this essay. Consequently they misunderstood what was happening and were often archaic in their attitudes because they related to a situation which had passed away. It can be said with some confidence that more progress in Christian social ethics has been made in the last fifty years than in the previous four hundred. By co-operative efforts the churches have brought themselves up to date. They are able to know what is happening and not be out of date. They have access to as much careful forecasting as is available. How fast and how far they will act upon it in their representative assemblies, at the level of local congregational activities, and in the activities of laymen in their different occupations, is another matter.

— 7 —

Reflections on Theologies of Social Change[1]

I

The Ecumenical Movement has been of immense importance
for Christian social ethics. Indeed it would not be too much to
say that the churches have made more progress in social ethics in
the last half century than since the break-up of medieval society.
It is because the search for the *renewal* as well as the unity of the
church has been at the heart of the Ecumenical Movement that
this progress has been made. One aspect of the quest for renewal
has been a determined effort to investigate what exactly is going
on in the world, so that the churches understand the situation of
their own day, and do not go on preaching and teaching and
formulating their priorities either oblivious of what is happening
or misunderstanding it. The churches were caught out in this
way when what is commonly called the industrial revolution
began to accelerate social change in Britain, with effects that
have become cumulative and world-wide. They had little or
nothing relevant to say at the time and have been slow to catch
up since. Pioneers in the Ecumenical Movement wanted to avert
the same mistake at a time of new social changes and pressures
in this century. This has meant that traditional theologies, confessional or not, all of which took shape in ages when social
change was so slow as to be almost imperceptible from one
generation to the next, have had to be refashioned to cope with
rapid social change. For, as we all know, social change is now so
rapid that it is extremely hard for the next generation to take
over from the previous one. Fathers and sons, for instance, find
it hard to understand one another, because their formative

experiences in their teenage years have been in such different circumstances.

The Oxford Conference on 'Church, Community and State' in 1937 was an attempt to cope with twentieth-century social change. In a sense it did so defensively against the challenge to the Christian faith of political totalitarianism; with concern for mass unemployment in the economic sphere not far behind. It produced theological insights of very high quality which are by no means exhausted. The Geneva Conference of 1966 on 'Christians in the Social and Technological Revolutions of our Time', which was deliberately planned to be a successor to Oxford in the new circumstances of the mid-sixties, was more on the offensive in its desire for Christian initiatives to influence the processes of social change, which were now taken for granted. It was no longer necessary to urge that theology take social change seriously, to point out that all previous theologies of any influence in all the main confessions, whether emanating from monasteries, seminaries or universities, had taken the *status quo* too seriously, and had thanked God for 'creation, *preservation* and all the blessings of this life' but not for change, whether evolutionary or revolutionary. At Geneva the mood was very different. It was there that a major ecumenical Christian conference outside Latin America first heard of a theology of revolution. It was there that the rapid social changes being brought about everywhere by the ongoing technological changes in the 'Western' world were faced. At the same time the protest against them by many of the affluent youth in that world began to be heard. It was at Geneva, too, that the break-up of the monolithic Marxist world was registered, and with it the rising expectations of the politically decolonialized Third World, and their sharp criticisms of the wealthy world.

Since the Geneva Conference we have seen a very marked growth of theologies of social change. The term 'political theology' has been coined. Within it there have been theologies of development, of revolution and of liberation; and there has been Black theology, which is also essentially one of social change. They are all related to theologies of hope; and in all the emphasis is much more on terrestrial than on celestial hopes. They are clearly vigorous and important. Indeed I do not think that nearly enough attention has been paid to them in Britain. Nevertheless I also think that some cautions need to be expressed about them. This essay is an attempt to reflect on Christian social responsibility in the last quarter of the twentieth century in the light of these recent developments. Working on the assumption that it is the continued advances in pure science and technology that bring in their train economic, social and political changes, it begins by giving a rough sketch of what is going on in the world, with particular stress on the industrial West, of which Britain is a part, and the problems it raises for us. These problems are seen to be essentially political ones; and as Christian insights need to be brought alongside empirical situations if they are to guide, fortify and inspire us, an examination of the contribution of these political theologies naturally follows after the sketch of the empirical situation. But as they all give a decisive place to New Testament data the essay, before examining them, looks at the New Testament teaching on Christian hope, and then asks how far these political theologies have used that teaching in an illuminating way in spelling out Christian social and political responsibilities and choices in our time.

II

A mood of pessimism has overtaken the Western world after an unprecedented twenty-five years of economic growth and the comparative optimism of the mid-sixties. This is partly due to the shock caused by the power exercised by the oil producers of OPEC over oil prices and supplies (the first time the affluent world has been treated in a way it has been accustomed to treat others). But it is also due to our inability to control inflation, which had been occasioned, well before the dramatic rise in the price of oil, by the rise in food prices as a result of bad harvests in Russia and India. It showed how dependent the whole world is on each part and on the weather; even the affluent, though much less vulnerable, cannot entirely insulate themselves. A third

reason for pessimism is that the affluent have become more aware
of the social ills in their own countries, which with all their
wealth they have failed to solve.

Nevertheless we must not be too impressed by what is probably a temporary mood. There may be economic and social
disaster ahead; and of course should a major war break out the
disaster is scarcely calculable. However, international relations
is not the theme of this essay, and it will assume that a major
war will not break out. In that case the material resources and
scientific skills of the affluent world are so great that it is likely
that the immediate economic problems will reach a tolerable
solution in three or four years' time, and that the underlying
factors which have been in operation in the last few decades
(and some of them far longer) will still operate. In particular,
through the continued development of pure science and technology the processes of economic growth and rapid social
change will continue.

From this angle human history was one of relative stagnation
until about the year 1760. Since then we have seen an ever
increasing control of matter and energy, and a steady long-
term growth of the economy at an over-all rate of not less than
3% p.a. GNP. The affluent world is more and more deliberately
organizing knowledge by creating the intellectual tools for
grasping and deliberately changing the world. We are often
told that 50% of all the natural scientists who ever lived are
alive now. We are also told that organized innovation is 99%
sweat and 1% genius. We shall, therefore, expect to see an increased speed in the application of technical discoveries. Recently there has been a breakthrough in processing information by
computers, and we are on the edge of a breakthrough in distributing it by computerized learning processes and telecom-
munications by satellites. Our powers of calculations have
increased by a factor of 10,000 in the last fifteen years, and at a
rapidly falling cost. In many sciences knowledge doubles in ten
years. In some, four-fifths of what will be relevant knowledge at
the turn of the century is not yet known. Man's age-old economic problem of the scarcity of basic food, clothing and shelter

for the bulk of the world's population may be in sight of solution in perhaps fifty years; the equivalent of the sound barrier in this matter can be broken. This is vital to about 2,300 millions of the 3,600 million people now alive. But whether they *will* benefit from the growing affluence of the technologically advanced world is a fundamental question addressed first to us who live in it.

None of this will happen without difficulties. I mention three.

1. First of all there is difficulty in forecasting developments in any one science, let alone its interaction with other sciences. Kahn and Weiner in their study of *The Year 2000* mention a survey of the future made in 1937 which missed atomic energy, the computer, antibiotics, radar and jet propulsion. The problem is that established knowledge is itself a conservative force, and that the absorption and even retrieval of it becomes a daunting task. Also, few of us have new ideas after the age of twenty-five. In short, it is extremely hard to look ahead more than fifteen years with any confidence; and if in economic terms the future is discounted by 10% p.a., that too means that little weight is given to more than fifteen years ahead. Certainly we need to think ahead as efficiently as we can, but it is unlikely that we can project with much certainty beyond fifteen years, a length of time when a great deal can in fact change. If I am told, for example, that the world's iron reserves as at present known will be exhausted at present trends of consumption in ninety-three years I am unimpressed; there are too many imponderable factors in that time scale. We cannot be responsible for a future we cannot foresee.

2. Next there is the difficulty of forecasting the use which will be made of discoveries. The German chemist who a hundred years ago compounded polystyrene had no thought that it could be used to make a superior napalm, enabling it to stick more effectively to its victims. This difficulty is a fact of life with which we have to live, endeavouring to be responsible in our own generation and leaving it to succeeding ones to face their responsibilities. In our time we have to face the

fact that the explosion of knowledge since 1940 has been such that our monitoring devices and safeguards have proved inadequate, so that we can no longer take clean air, earth and water for granted. This is the truth in the ecological controversy of the last few years; and the problems to which it has drawn attention are beginning to be tackled. Although much depends on international co-operation, and progress is patchy and hazardous, there is no reason to suppose they will not be tackled, at least to a reasonable extent. Beyond this the demand for a 'stable state', that is to say the end of economic growth, is a mistake. In a nutshell it depends upon an argument that we are using up irreplaceable natural resources because population is increasing exponentially (that is to say at a constant rate over time), and therefore so is the rate of consumption and pollution. It ignores the fact that technological innovation is also increasing, and this is affecting all the other variables. The need is rather to use economic growth to cope with the necessities of the people already born (whilst doing what we can to reduce birth rates). We must not be deflected from removing crippling poverty from over half the world's population.

3. A political difficulty emerges from these other ones. The complexities and uncertainties of decision-making require the continual feedback of information and re-ordering of priorities. This in turn requires a very sophisticated decision-making process just at the time when more and more people are rightly wanting to participate in it. A high degree of political wisdom will be needed to cope with this. Indeed what speed of change can political institutions themselves cope with? Western-type political democracies do not find it easy to cope with rapid change. If governments demand it they are likely to be voted out of office. And how much change can people stand? How malleable and mobile can they be? What institutions are needed to help them to face change? The answer to these questions is not clear, and they suggest caution; but if ordered change is not secured a dangerous backlog builds up which leads to social explosion.

At this point we note the rejection of the technologically affluent future by many of the younger generation. The cry of the Paris students in 1968 was 'death to the technical reason' and 'all power to the imagination'. To many of the student generation the rich of our age appear poor and detestable. They reject what appears to be the likely future of a mass consumption society. They have a sense of alienation in the midst of abundance. They seek a non-competitive communal life. In one sense it is ironical that they are bored by the affluence which their parents have created and which they have enjoyed, since it is the basis of a welfare state which enables them to opt out whilst being able to presuppose a level of basic securities below which they will not be allowed to fall. Yet it is a healthy sign that concern for the quality of life comes to the fore once a certain standard of living has been reached, provided it does not turn aside from the task of seeing that the majority of the world's population can experience what the students can take for granted as underpinning them. The control of technological power and the use of the resources it provides remain the key issue. It is a *political* one, not a technological one. There must be no turning back on the political task.

III

In many respects the Communist world is similar to the West in basic economic and technological background. Starting a long way back in economic development, governments which cannot be removed from office by the electorate have been able to impose a rate of forced saving on their populations which the electorates of the Western world would not tolerate. So they have had a very rapid economic growth. The same difficulties have to be faced as in the West and, all in all, the Communist world is neither more nor less successful in solving them than we are. Again some of the younger generation are disenchanted with the quality of life they find and are expected to look forward to; and a significant number of the older generation also question whether the material transformation of which Marx spoke is enough to satisfy human aspirations. There has been something of a break-up in monolithic Marxism, and a cautious improvement in the conditions for the flourishing of the human spirit. Under the utopian theory that once the advance guard of the workers has seized power all *fundamental* political problems are solved, the tactical struggles which inevitably accompany bids for power in the political processes are interpreted as counter-revolutionary moves, and repressions and purges have been the result. Now these are somewhat abated, but there is no clear alternative explanation of political processes. Marxism in China is clearly making an effort to avoid Russian fossilization, and it is a source of inspiration for many in the Third World who have no time for the Russian version of Marxism. China is also a country with a pronounced this-worldly orientation, and without the secularized biblical undertones which are unmistakable in Soviet Marxism. For these reasons the theological significance of Maoist China is a question of the first importance, but not one which can be pursued further here.

When we turn to the Third World it has now become necessary to separate the newly rich oil states from the rest. For our present purposes we need say no more about them, but turn to what now is being called the Fourth World. Asia, Africa and Latin America differ in important respects from one another, but these differences will be ignored in my brief comment. Here the speed of change is even more traumatic, as traditional societies are hit by the effects of the technology of the West without the infrastructure of social and political institutions which developed in the latter in the last century. Tribalism and the caste system are instances of additional complications. Half of the population is under twenty-nine, and it is set against authoritarian and bureaucratic structures and restlessly in search of a new future, broadly intepreted as a socialism of self-management. Awareness of the growing economic disparities between their world and the rest has led to a growing demand for a greater share of affluence, and a more fundamental demand for liberation from oppressive power structures, both neo-colonial and domestic, and by force if necessary. In Latin

America the search for a new society is related to the process of 'conscientization' by which those on the margin of society become self-conscious of themselves and their state of life in the act of grasping that change is possible and of moving themselves towards changing it. Meanwhile the influx into the cities of the Fourth World is becoming a cascade. Driven from the villages where there is no work, people settle in the shanty towns on the edge of the cities where there is also no work, and where the social restraints of village life no longer hold. This is perhaps the most potentially explosive social factor of all.

How can the Fourth World exert enough pressure on the other worlds to secure that the vast resources of those worlds are used towards a more just international economic and social order? It seems clear that the comfortable do not take seriously the burden of rectifying injustices until the under-privileged both become articulate and have enough strength to make a dint on them. The Fourth World has become articulate, but it is in a weak position against the other worlds whose economic and technological power gets relatively greater against theirs. In the long term a humane and just world is a gain for all, but in the short term the wealthy are only too likely not to see beyond their immediate interests. Will they learn in time?

At any rate in the West, governments are influenced by their electorates and respond to pressures. It is also in the West that Christians are strongest and still represent in most countries a significant element in the electorate. Is it possible that they could become more alert and informed and thus politically more effective? What theological resources have they for coping with social change? And what are their hopes for the future? We are now offered the various political theologies of hope and change, all relating themselves to the New Testament. Therefore it is to my own understanding of New Testament hopes and their significance that I refer before reflecting on the various political theologies.

IV

New Testament thinking is both eschatological and apocalyptic.

Eschatology is concerned with the 'last' events in time in the sense of those which are of lasting and ultimate significance for the whole; apocalyptic is concerned with the end of ongoing or routine time. Both carry on categories of thought which are of central significance in the Old Testament. The key to the ministry of Jesus (in word and deed) is its eschatological character. He presented his hearers with a challenge to moral and religious discernment; those who had eyes to see were to realize that the hoped-for 'last days' in the Jewish religious tradition, when Yahweh would vindicate his purposes, had already dawned in his own ministry, paradoxical as is was, since, while in some respects it fulfilled Old Testament hopes, in others it negated them. The powers of the 'last days' were thus already at work in the world. At the same time it is very likely that Jesus had a foreshortened expectation of the future of routine time, that is to say that he had a lively apocalyptic expectation that it would soon come to an end with a *parousia*, when the eschatological powers now already at work in the ongoing world would achieve an evident triumph, of which his own ministry was a proleptic indication. The earliest Christian community certainly had his double eschatological and apocalyptic outlook. It had no doubt that 'the light of the knowledge of the glory of God' had been seen 'in the face of Jesus Christ' (II Cor. 4.6); that in a decisive sense it was living in a new age; that the powers of the age to come were already at work. Yet the present age still continued, though not (it was believed) for long. Soon would come the *parousia*, the return of Christ, and the end of the present time series. The early Christians lived with the sense of membership in a new community of the Spirit, based on faith in Christ, love to God and to one another through him, and hope for the imminent final triumph of what Jesus had begun. They lived in the two ages at once; they lived between the kingdom of God drawing near in Jesus and its soon-to-be-accomplished consummation.

The Christian's hope in the New Testament is of the final triumph of good over evil, that is to say the abolition of sin; the final triumph of the new life in Christ over human finitude, that is to say the abolition of death; and the fullness of love, joy and peace, that is to say the end of that boring aspect of routine time which is so pungently expressed in the book Ecclesiastes. This hope is epitomized in the thought of being 'with Christ' and of having a new resurrection 'body'; and thus it transcends what is within history and continuous with our space and time, and apocalyptically looks to what is discontinuous with it and with our bodies with their present space and time equipment. There is an inescapable 'other-worldly' stress in the New Testament. But this is in no way to be confused with the Platonic idea that this world is only a shadow of the real world. In both Testaments *olam* and *aion* are used both for this age and the coming one.

Christian hope lies between ignorance and knowledge. It neither indulges in unnecessary curiosity, for example about the date of 'the end', nor does it wait passively on events. It eagerly grasps adumbrations of the new age already experienced and is active and eager in its outlook. In hoping for what we do not yet see we show our endurance (Rom. 8.25), but it is much more than a passive endurance. What we already know of the eschatologically ultimate in Christ is the basis of our future expectations; we are betrothed and we look to the marriage; we are eschatologically renewed and we look for the *parousia*.

In almost all the New Testament these hopes are fore-shortened, so that there is no hope for the terrestrial future. The existing institutions of society, notably slavery, are accepted and humanized within the Christian community with no thought of change. In St John's gospel, however, a drastic theological reconsideration has taken place. The imminent apocalyptic expectation has gone, but the radical eschatological Christian outlook is no whit diminished – if anything the radical contrast between its light and the surrounding darkness is intensified — and is left as the permanent possession of the church through indefinite ongoing chronological time. It was of immense importance that this theological shift took place when it became clear that no imminent *parousia* was likely. But its effect on immediate decision-making is negligible. The Christians are to continue with the same active eager attitude to chronological time, and they are to continue to grasp adumbrations of the new age as before. Whether there is only a little routine time or a lot – scores or hundreds or thousands of years – makes no difference. Each day is an occasion of joyful response to the eschatological nearness brought about by Christ.

Apocalyptic is a dispensable thought-form. This means that Christians should have a positive and forward-looking attitude to the future, that they should have criteria for judging in which direction they wish to influence it, and that they should be on the look-out for all signs of renewal as judged by these criteria. But it does not mean that they have any clear picture of what is to happen in the course of chronological time. They have no grounds for *a priori* theological pessimism which thinks that little or nothing can be done, or that things will get worse. No limits have been set by God to human achievement if humanity responds to his call and is sensitive to human need. Neither are there grounds for *a priori* theological optimism. There is no assurance that humanity will become more obedient, or that there is any built-in process leading to a better world. There may be catastrophes; or perhaps a series of renewals and catastrophes. This is because each generation has to make its own the moral advances made by its predecessor, and if possible extend them. If it fails at least to do the former, the disastrous effect of the collapse of something superior is more than that of something less so. Moreover, the subtler temptations arise out of genuine moral achievements. A society which presupposes co-operation and fails to get it is worse off than one that appeals overwhelmingly to self-interest, as *laissez-faire* did. That was what was so shocking about the regress to synthetic technological barbarism in Nazi Germany. Social change (unlike biological evolution) can be rapid but it is also precarious. Good and evil may well grow together until the end of time. What we know of the recalcitrance of human beings makes us cautious, just as what we know of their potentialities of goodness makes us hopeful. But the basic ground of our hope, and in the Christian outlook hope vastly outweighs gloom, is in what we already know and have experienced through Jesus. It leads to the affirmation that history will not ultimately defeat God's purpose (but not that that purpose will be achieved in the continuities of our present historical order), and that no human effort to work for the good of humanity is wasted.

To repeat, our hope in Christ does not give any detailed content to our hope for our terrestrial future, though it gives us ground for taking that future seriously and positively. It is true that there has been much spurious other-worldliness in the Christian tradition, and this has given plausibility to the Marxist criticism of it; but finally the Christian hope is 'other-worldly' in the sense that its fulfilment transcends this world. This is important in a future-orientated society which may easily be tempted, as Marxism is, to inflict cruelties on the present generation in the interests of future ones. Aldous Huxley once said that a future-orientated society without a hope of heaven would be a tyranny. It is just because we have no abiding city that we can laugh rather than sigh, and that we must take the needs of our present fellow-members of the earthly city so seriously.

The Christian emphasis is on the call to be obedient today within the perspective of the future that can be reasonably foreseen. Man 'come of age' has great powers and great responsibilities under God. He is not bound by the past but free for the future; he is liberated to commit himself to the world in hope and to look for the common grace and the hidden grace at work in it. Fear of the unknown future is a major obstacle to making a creative response to a time of rapid change. This is particularly acute in affluent societies who are conscious of what they have to lose; their heart is where their treasure is. It is all the more serious if Christians are timid and fearful. Instead they should discern hope in the midst of the struggle for human conditions without giving way to zealotry or escapism. Of course it is possible to have courage without hope, and we must honour many humanists who possess it. It is possible to have fanatical hopes, and these need mitigating by a dose of Christian realism. It is also possible to be quietist and 'other-worldly', and this needs correcting by a lively Christian hope as a source of vision and strength in facing the human future.

V

What I have just written has some affinities with the political theologies of the last ten years, but it would by no means be accepted by them in its entirety. But first of all we need to understand what is meant by the term 'political theology', which I take to be in itself a witness to an important truth. Negatively it is a protest against the 'privatization' of theology; positively it is not so much a 'theology of politics' as we might have one of industry, or art, or education or sport, but rather an assertion that politics is not a *part* of theology which one may or may not engage in according to one's choice. To think theologically is willy-nilly a political activity, whether one is conscious of it or not. This is because *all* thinking takes place in a social context; and the social and the political realm overlap to a considerable extent. It is true that in some aspects of theological study, textual criticism for example, the influence of the social context is negligible. In descriptive studies, historical and contemporary, it has more place. To understand the Chalcedonian formula one has to understand its vocabulary, and that arose in a social context; St Anselm on the doctrine of the atonement is unintelligible without a knowledge of feudalism. As each generation rewrites history with questions, insights and perspectives occasioned by its own situation, so the church continually reflects on her own past and sees it in new ways. 'The faith once delivered to the saints' (Jude 3) is seen very differently at different times. When we come to think theologically in our own time, the political context of that thought is inescapable. To think we can be neutral is a delusion; it is impossible to escape out of our milieu and to avoid conditioning factors, as if we could be 'pure' reasoners, with reasoning in pure mathematics as the model in our minds. Of course we can be partially aware of conditioning factors and partially overcome them, but not completely so. Moreover the political realm is one of conflicts of groups and institutions, from which churches are not exempt and which Christians cannot escape. The importance of the Ecumenical Movement is that it makes us relate our thinking to that of

Christians and churches from different contexts (often adding also the vividness which comes from personal encounter) within the fellowship of the whole church, so that we may learn from one another and make a more adequate response to the issues that face us, holding inevitable conflicts within a deeper commitment to the crucified and risen Christ.

There can be no dichotomy in the Christian task between changing persons and changing structures. This is a false antithesis which never quite dies down. Even the most 'personal' preaching of the gospel requires an interpretation which itself is in a social-political context; and structures of life (family, work, citizenship) mould persons from their infancy onwards, so that the way they work cannot be left unexamined. In an important sense theology is inescapably political. Those who have stressed this have also stressed how often it has conformed to the *status quo*, or imagined it was neutral and a-political (even in the case of a man like Charles de Foucauld), and how little it has challenged current structures. They ask whether this is true to the stance of the biblical data, once the time-bound situation of the early church is allowed for.

The theology of hope has been a pervasive political theology in the last decade or so. It does not stress faith in God's past actions so much as hope for his eschatological action in history in the future. It professes to empower the lives of Christians from the end or fulfilment of history with an eschatological vision of a fulfilled kingdom of God, as the basis for breaking up existing social and political structures and establishing new ones; and also for keeping perseverance and hope alive in defeats (for it is not blindly optimistic). It criticizes a stress on present eschatology as leading to a bourgeois and spurious other-worldly individualism. In doing so it undoubtedly has the kind of personal pietism associated with Bultmann in mind, with its stress on an inward relation to God and the realization of an authentic but a-historical self. This, however, is an over-simplification. Ethics has never been a main interest of Bultmann; he has little to say about it, and that of limited use. There is no necessity for a stress on present eschatology to have that

effect. The Berrigan brothers, for instance, or Bishop Colin
Winter, find the roots of their hopes in the presence of Christ in
the eucharist, and from this derive their challenge to established
structures. Moreover, those who have in fact most stressed future
eschatology in Christian history have generally thought of it in
very individualistic terms: 'salvation for my soul after death'. In
fact both present and future eschatological emphases can be
subject to individualistic distortions and the neglect of social
change and social justice.

On the other hand the theology of hope is in danger of its own
characteristic distortion, a utopian strain, to which I shall turn
shortly. But it need not be. Indeed on occasions it does warn
against canonizing *any* order, even as it stresses the infinite
possibilities of the open future. But on whether its projected
transformation of the world is to be part of, and continuous
with, our human history or not, it appears to be ambiguous.
More important still is that with its stress on looking for the
radically new from God as 'the power of the future', quite unlike
what we know of the present or of human potentialities so far, it
fails to make clear how what is radically new in the future can
guide ethical action now. Rather, we can only base ourselves on
our *present* understanding of the *past*. This is not to say that we
are in bondage to either the past or the present, but we are compelled to go back for our criteria today to what we know now of
the revelation in Christ. In fact when we come to what the
theologies of hope say about the present we find they are wrestling with the same problems as others, with no clearer or agreed
answers (for example to the problem of violence). They express
a change of mood, and one which when not utopian is positive
and valuable, but otherwise a great deal of the theology of hope
seems to involve the moving of biblical material in a different
pattern without much greater theological illumination. It seems
an involved way of urging Christians to take the future seriously
and work to make it more just and human. It is still too much a
theology of the Word, in the aftermath of Karl Barth, attempt-
ing to move too directly from scripture to the modern world.
Scriptural revelation does not tell us of our terrestrial future;

from it we can derive an attitude to and criteria for dealing with the different foreseeable futures that different generations and societies have to face. The call is for joyful obedience today; the materials for decision comes from the empirical data of the day.

Some theologians of hope stress the importance of apocalyptic for expressing confidence in the completion of the disclosures of God's triumph at the end of history. This may be only a question of the terms in which convictions are expressed rather than of their content, but in view of the importance of the distinction between eschatology and apocalyptic in the New Testament, and the fact that the distinction between present (or realized) and future eschatology is a good way of expressing the Christian hope, it seems better to abandon apocalyptic as a category no longer useful in Christian theology, especially since as inherited in the Christian tradition it has had some serious drawbacks. (i) It has laid too much claim to precise knowledge of the future in God's intentions, continually forecasting the date of the *parousia*, and not being willing enough to live by faith. (ii) It has had a pessimistic view of history, assuming that things would get worse before Yahweh intervened to sort out the mess and vindicate his faithful. (iii) It has not attached much importance in any case to the ongoing events in human history in view of the expected cataclysmic future. (iv) Its hopes for an absolutely new future have been too discontinuous with the ongoing events in human history. (v) Believers have been too certain of their place in the new post-apocalyptic order, and too certain that it is an exclusive place. There is a hope for the 'nations' in the New Testament; and the more conscious we become of the plural nature of the world, and the greater the insight we attain into other religions and philosophies, the more we are coming to see a relation to Christ in them, even though they are unaware of or would deny it.

VI

From the theology of hope has come the theology of liberation, whose provenance has been Latin America, even though its ingredients are all European. It has many merits. It takes seriously the injustice and oppression in the world about which traditional theologies have been far too complacent. It stresses the violence embedded in existing structures in which theology has been too ready to acquiesce. It sees that technological development can easily reinforce these injustices. It wants to rouse those on the margin of society to realize their own potentiality in envisaging social change and taking steps to bring it about; in doing so they will express love to their oppressors by liberating them from the alienating effects of their own oppression. It stresses that neutrality is impossible when considering social injustices; and that it is necessary to find the sufferings of others intolerable and be willing to forgo a clinging to personal innocence, and to bear the toils and conflicts needed to remove them. It calls for a quickening of imagination to envisage social goals which are more precise than a utopia and less so than a technically developed model (which it thinks will be too conservatively influenced by the present).

However, some cautions need to be expressed. (1) In practice it adopts without arguing for it a Marxist or neo-Marxist social, economic and political analysis. This seems to be considered self-evidently correct, but the assumption needs defence. It can hardly be a *theological* judgment that Marxism is the 'scientific' political and social analysis. Therefore it must be argued out in political and social terms. In the trivial sense that 'we are all Marxists now', in much the same way as we are all Darwinians or Freudians now, the assumption is justified. But in a more rigorous sense it is not. The Marxist theories all embody useful insights, but each one taken separately, and the whole lot taken together, are sufficiently defective as a basis for prediction (which is the point of claiming to be a scientific theory) to provide a very unsafe ground for action. This is not least because Marxism is clearly related to the nineteenth-century state of British and West European thought and society out of which it grew (aware of conditioning factors in all other thought except its own). To justify this verdict is not possible within this essay; all that can be done here is to draw attention to the assumption about Marxism so widely found in theologians of liberation.

Gutierrez, for instance, writes of the need for a 'scientific' approach in order to discover laws proper to the political world which will give revolutionary activity effectiveness, and assumes he has found that approach in Marxism. To him it provides a science of the facts but lacks mobilizing force; whilst Christianity is a faith which nerves to action by providing an imaginative utopia of a society without class and liberated from all oppressors.

The Movement of Christians for Socialism, which met in Santiago in 1972 at the time of the UNCTAD Conference and not long before the overthrow of the Allende Government, said, 'Today an awareness is growing of a strategic alliance between Christian revolutionaries and Marxist revolutionaries in the liberation process' and refers to 'walking in common' towards 'a common global historical liberation process'. In the Philippines, Fr Luis Jalandoni, the son of a wealthy landed family, was captured in September 1972 after being on the run for a year with the New People's Army, the military wing of the Communist Party, in the struggle against President Marcos. He had been working for basic trade union rights for poor sugar workers against sugar planters with their own private armies, and had got nowhere. He became convinced that only armed struggle could avail and so he threw in his lot with the Marxists. I quote him rather than the better known Fr Camilo Torres. But there are many others. From these examples one can see why the Marxist analysis appeals, but that does not of itself mean that it is correct. We can also see why one might ally with Marxists for tactical reasons, not 'scientific' ones. However, it is these latter that theologies of liberation advance.

(2) There are strong messianic and utopian strains in these theologies which need to be called into question. The projecting of the pervasive New Testament language of the 'new' on to the political future leads in many of these theologies to an explicit emphasis on a messianic hope, held in what is described as the revolutionary present, for a qualitatively new future which will transfigure politics and involve a fundamental transformation of history. Rubem Alves, for instance, makes much of a distinction

between humanist messianism (by which he means Marxism) and a Christian messianic humanism.[2] There is a frequent appeal to the saga of the exodus. Gutierrez says it points to a unity between the social-political and the redemptive dimensions of life which was fulfilled and deepened in Christ. There are not two histories, one sacred and one profane, but one history in which God acts in a way of which the exodus saga is the model.[3] This ignores the fact that there is a vital difference between the two Testaments at this point. In the Old Testament there is one kingdom which is both church and state. The theme of the Old Testament is the formation of a people of God which in some sense or other has an universal mission, but which is centred in the Jewish state in the various forms it took in the Old Testament period; that is why no attention is given to those who were driven out of their lands in order that the people of God might occupy them. In the New Testament there are two kingdoms. The people of God has been reconstituted; it has broken the bounds of the Jewish state and has become in principle universal. Christians now live in two kingdoms, two cities (Augustine), two realms (Luther), not one. In the kingdom of God the messianic role has been accomplished in the ministry of Jesus. It is quite illegitimate to transfer it to various movements in the kingdom(s) of the world. God's action in history (to use in passing a term which needs careful explication) is providential, not messianic; his rule in history is more hidden and history more ambiguous than biblical messianism would suggest. In spite of the exodus saga the people of God found themselves in exile; and revolutions can be counter-revolutionary! A strain in Zionism which holds still to the one kingdom view adds dangerous religious dimensions to an already strong nationalist fervour in Israel.

This messianism is one aspect of a tendency to move directly from biblical categories to the modern world in a way which is dangerously *simpliste*. It obscures the need to come to terms with empirical evidence *en route*, and leads to the absolutizing of current positions in political ethics. It moves too easily to and fro between biblical symbols and motives on the one hand and interpretations of current history and commitments to political programmes on the other. It is a legacy to some current political theology of biblical theology out of the Calvinist tradition of using scripture. An examination of Puritan preaching in the twelve months after the execution of Charles I shows innumerable sermons being preached on Psalm 149.8, which refers to 'binding their kings in chains and their nobles with links of iron', transferring the text to the current situation in a way which seems foolish now, but is being paralleled in much of the recent theologies of change. Much Black theology, for instance, thinks of Blacks as a 'chosen people' because they are oppressed, transferring the category from the Bible to where it does not apply, and adding a dangerously uncritical messianic overtone to a proper concern for social justice, a concern which would be even better if it showed more awareness of other oppressed groups of other colours and situations.

(3) Utopian strains are found in the theology of liberation which are closely related to messianic ones. The classical discussion of utopias in the last forty years has been that of Karl Mannheim. There is an interesting ambiguity in his book *Ideology and Utopia* at this point, arising from the fact that the different sections of the book were originally written in German at different times. The main thrust is a cool dissection of ideologies as the rationalizations of privileged social groups and classes, and of utopias as those of unprivileged classes. In effect to set them in a social context by the techniques of the sociology of knowledge is to remove some of their absolute character, when their purpose is in fact to evoke precisely that character for those who hold to them. Yet Mannheim also holds that utopias are necessary or men will not have the vision and drive to produce a more humane society, so that 'man would lose his ability to shape history and therewith his ability to understand it' (p. 236). So utopias are both in a sense deceitful and yet necessary. Reinhold Niebuhr came to a similar conclusion in his earlier writings which were more influenced by a Marxist analysis; at the end of his *Moral Man and Immoral Society*, he hoped that the workers would retain their illusionary dream of perfect

justice long enough to overthrow the worst oppression of the present. 'The illusion is dangerous because it encourages terrible fanaticisms. It must therefore be brought under the control of reason. One can only hope that reason will not destroy it before its work is done' (p. 277). The remark needs some qualification in any case as a political generalization, but the question for the Christian is, are Christian hopes of a kind already mentioned not enough, or do we need misleading utopias as well to move us to forward-looking action?

Using the term in a different sense from Mannheim, Christians are often urged by theologians of liberation to develop ideologies for action; to grasp our environment with active systems of hope-filled meaning and to commit ourselves to the action they call for. The influence of the Marxist Ernst Bloch has been great at this point. His *Das Prinzip Hoffnung* (1959) has regrettably not been translated into English, for it lies behind a good deal of liberation theology. His challenge is to 'dream forward' as a cognitive act; to push beyond the 'objective possibilities' – that is, everything which can reasonably be expected or cannot be excluded by present evidence – to the 'real possibilities' yet to mature, since they will grow out of a new reality. Moltmann urges us not to be hamstrung in our hopes for a desirable future by the constriction of a calculable future based on extrapolations from the present.[4] The danger of utopianism in such exhortations needs guarding against. It leads to the despising of precise goals and the presentation of impossibilities as possibilities; it leads to the atmosphere of holy wars. If utopian movements are successful they are likely to lead to tyranny because of their claim to embody a greater perfection than the facts warrant, and if unsuccessful to ever greater repression by the powers that be. The refusal to pay attention to the evidence of the present quickly leads to anti-intellectualism and to stereotyped judgments. There is enough of both in the world without Christians adding to them. Yet in saying this I am conscious that Christians too often will not sustain the slog of continued political effort unless a crusading utopian mood can be worked up. It is one of their biggest failures. For politics, to quote an anonymous reviewer, is a realm 'in which men of muddled motives and mixed ambitions have to make choices that threaten their principles, strain their affections and wear out their nerves'.

In order to sustain the ongoing political task deep commitment and reserves of patience, perseverance, courage, wisdom, hope – not to speak of faith and love – are needed. Men and women know something of these in their own lives by virtue of their sheer humanity, and on the basis of these qualities numbers of them have served their fellows in the political sphere. Those who are Christians should be even more alert in this realm, for their faith can be a source of further strength to them. All the virtues just referred to have a deep light shed on them by Christ; indeed it is what we know of them already which enables us to see how much they are deepened by him. Christians have greater resources to draw on through the 'new creation' brought about by Christ, and in particular they are given a commitment to the basic equality and fellowship of all men in Christ, which in itself continually calls in question accepted institutions, and issues in a particular concern for the poor and disadvantaged. Furthermore, vision and imagination is needed in order to understand both other people and social and political situations; it is not just a matter of a technical mastery of the 'facts', indispensable as that is. A wisdom beyond that is needed to assess their significance and context, in short, to understand a situation in depth. Also, it is necessary to create models to simplify the task of grasping with the mind a series of complex and varying phenomena. All this is true. But it is a long way from the call to ideologize or create utopias. It is vital to see things as they are to the best of our ability, making all allowances for conditioning factors, as the basis for seeing what is a realizable as well as a desirable future, in the direction of which we should try to move by the next steps which have to be taken. There are indeterminate possibilities for the future, but no utopia is on the way; moral ambiguities and precarious balances of power are a permanent human condition.

The utopian element in these theologies of social change is

closely related to their preoccupation with the Marxist analysis. In Marxism two elements are curiously related. One is the claim to be a 'scientific' theory of social change, to which I have already referred; the other is its utopian horizon in its picture of the coming classless society. Related to these is the curious tension in it between the 'scientific' theories which purport to uncover the dialectical power struggles through which social change will inevitably proceed until the classless society is reached, and the view that men should create for themselves and seize revolutionary opportunities to push the process on. Many liberation theologies exhibit the same dual attitude. They accept too easily the Marxist claim to be scientific, and at the same time say that Christianity and Marxism are congenial because both drive us to take hold of our future and heighten our powers to do so. (They also add very truly that Christianity also includes the dead in its hope, whereas Marxism cannot.) However, Marxism is of great importance for Christians, who need to see it as an 'unwitting servant of Yahweh', like the Assyrians and Babylonians and Cyrus in the Old Testament.[5] There is every reason to take the Marxist-Christian dialogue seriously and to be ready for it whenever the chance occurs. The period between the publication of Pope John XXIII's encyclical *Pacem in Terris*, when dialogue got seriously under way, and the Russian invasion of Czechoslovakia was brief. But sooner or later dialogue will be resumed. Some Marxists already see Christianity to be very different in principle from the spuriously other-worldly and individualistic forms of it which Marx and Engels and the break-up of monolithic Marxism is producing a community of questioning in many Marxist circles akin to that in Christian ones. When it comes, the Christians will have to try, with Pannenberg, to show the Marxists that human alienation requires a deeper cure than social change can provide. To put it in another way, Jesus liberated in his lifetime, liberates now, and will liberate in the future. The Christians must also show the Marxists that belief in the transcendent God does not cramp and restrain human possibilities but sustains and liberates them. They will be tempted in doing this tacitly to accept the

Marxist claim to be a 'scientific' analysis of the facts of the present, and will therefore be in danger of continually mistaken tactics based on a defective over-all analysis. But to criticize Marxism as 'scientific' can only be done in the political, social and economic context in which the analysis is expressed. There is no direct route from the Bible to it. This is a position no different from that in which the Christian is placed in respect to secular disciplines in general, for instance both the natural and social sciences. He needs to pay attention to them, and it is good that theologians are now taking them seriously, but they must beware of being swept along by intellectual fashions (which occur in every intellectual discipline), without examining more carefully how well they are founded. The inadequacies of the Club of Rome report on *The Limits to Growth* or *The Ecologist's* report, *A Blueprint for Survival*, to take two examples, can only be realized by participation in the debate they have provoked; there is no direct route from the Bible to the matter.

VII

Little needs to be added on the theologies of revolution. The word does not necessarily imply physical force, but rapid, radical and discontinuous change. Nevertheless force often accompanies political revolutions. The theologies of revolution join in pointing out that established theologies have far too readily sanctified the *status quo*. The preservative action of God has been overstressed. Now, however, consideration of criteria for just wars in modern conditions has been extended to those for just revolutions. But in changing the emphasis to God's concern for the poor and oppressed, and his activity in overthrowing the mighty out of their seats and exalting the poor and weak, greatly inflated claims for revolutions have been made. It is said that they are parabolic signs of the transfiguration of politics, bearers of a righteousness not their own, God's instruments for exposing the falsehoods in established structures, always more likely to have truth on their side than established patterns. Lehmann holds that the emphasis on law and order is a vast distortion, and that freedom always has priority over order under God as justice has over law. Here one distortion has produced its opposite, and theology, instead of illuminating the tensions and ambiguities within which human life has to be lived, has given an uncritical sanction to one side of the human situation.

The truth in this is that to be radically concerned with persons and for the humanization of the structures in which persons live is in an important sense a revolutionary stance. It means that Christians cannot be content with existing structures (unless they have strong reasons to believe that no better ones are possible at the moment), and that they need to work at theologies which have a built-in ability to cope with change, and which fortify them in the arduous task of making constructive use of the changes which in our world will be going on anyway. To think one can be a-political is in fact covertly to support the *status quo*. They need to bring love, joy and creativity to a world which is either too fearful of change or too cocksure about it, but not at the cost of falling a prey to a political innocence compounded of messianic and utopian illusions.

VIII

Although all the elements of these various political theologies are European in origin, none of them has yet made much impact on the British scene, though to some extent they find a hearing among Christians of student age. Yet in a world where our policies affect others all over the globe, and where in the Ecumenical Movement great progress has been made in mutual understanding in the last half century, it is disturbing to find British theology and church life so insular. It is not that the British churches and British Christians give the impression of being particularly alert and active with respect to their own political responsibilities in the light of rapid social change. Quite the contrary. Yet to ask that they pay more attention to these theologies, not least out of concern for what has seemed to so many Christians in the Fourth World to speak to their condition, is not to ask that they be accepted without criticism.

Queries must be put against their easy acceptance of the Marxist analysis as 'scientific', and their tendency to dismiss all queries of it as reactionary; the danger of their biblicism and utopianism need pointing out. But in doing this we are in no way impugning particular actions and stances taken by Christians in situations quite different from ours, which we cannot fully appreciate from outside. Rather we deal with our own situation. We must show why the Marxist 'scientific' analysis does not fit it, but only as a step in wrestling with an economic and political analysis which does fit, and which throws light on goals for the next fifteen years or so which need to be worked for. This is a theme for another essay.

These political theologies have had a powerful effect in opening the eyes of every part of the Ecumenical Movement, not least the 'Faith and Order' aspect of it, to political tasks which cannot be shirked. British Christians need this stimulus and should be grateful for it. For the rest the New Testament present (or inaugurated) and future eschatological perspective, liberated from the 'time-bound' apocalyptic elements which are there associated with it, is the best basis for political theology. Reinhold Niebuhr expressed this in his own characteristic way in 1952 in *The Irony of American History* (p. 54):

Nothing that is worth doing can be achieved in our lifetime, therefore we must be saved by hope. Nothing which is true or beautiful or good makes complete sense in any immediate context of history; therefore we must be saved by faith. Nothing we do, however virtuous, can be accomplished alone; therefore we must be saved by love. No virtuous act is quite as virtuous from the standpoint of our friend and foe as it is from our standpoint. Therefore we must be saved by the final form of love which is forgiveness.

There is a slight overstatement here in the first sentence, where if 'ultimately' were inserted before 'worth doing' it would be less open to misunderstanding. Nevertheless this is a better theological horizon within which to work at a positive and forward-looking theology of social change, than that advanced in most of the political theologies of the last decade.

Notes

1. Christian Critiques of Capitalism Reconsidered

1. The first and present holder of the Chair is Canon Gordon Dunstan, to whose work over the years I am much indebted.

2. Then the holder of the Chair of Moral and Pastoral Theology in that University.

3. The more significant contributions to the discussion in the English-speaking world since Tawney's lecture are:

Josiah Stamp, *The Christian Ethic as an Economic Factor*, 1926
— *Motive and Method in a Christian Order*, 1936
— *Christianity and Economics*, 1939
A. D. Lindsay, *Christianity and Economics*, 1934
William Temple, *Christianity and Social Order*, 1942
F. H. Knight and T. W. Merriam, *The Economic Order and Religion*, 1948
John Sleeman, *Basic Economic Problems*, 1953
— *Economic Crisis: a Christian Perspective*, 1976
Denys Munby, *Christianity and Economic Problems*, 1956
— *God and the Rich Society*, 1961
Charles Elliott, *Inflation and the Compromised Church*, 1975
J. P. Wogaman, *Christians and the Great Economic Debate*, 1977
The Oxford Ecumenical Conference on Church, Community and State, 1937: Report, *The Churches Survey Their Task*, ed. J. H. Oldham, 1937, esp. Section 3, 'Church, Community and State in Relation to the Economic Order'.
A. Dudley Ward (ed.), *Goals of Economic Life*, 1953, and John Bennett and others, *Christian Values and Economic Life*, 1954 (two volumes of a six-volume report sponsored by the Federal Council of Churches of the USA).
Geneva Conference of the World Council of Churches on Church and Society, July 1966: Report, *Christians in the Technical and Social Revolution of our Time*, WCC 1967, esp. Section 1, 'Economic Growth in World Perspectives'. Also the essays in a preliminary volume, *Economic Development in World Perspective*, ed. Denys Munby, SCM Press and Association Press 1966.
The most important Roman Catholic thought is found in *Gaudium et Spes* (the Pastoral Constitution of the Second Vatican Council, 1965, often known as 'The Church in the Modern World'), the Papal Encyclicals *Mater et Magistra*, 1961 (John XXIII) and *Populorum*

Progressio, 1967 (Paul VI), and in the Apostolic Letter *Octogesima Adveniens*, 1971 (Paul VI).

4. D. G. MacRae in a review, concerned with Max Weber, in *The Times Higher Educational Supplement*, 3 June 1977.

5. See Dietrich Bonhoeffer, *Letters and Papers from Prison*, the letters of 8 June and 16 July 1944, 3rd ed. revised and enlarged, 1971, pp. 324–9 and 357–61.

6. A good example of this is John Wesley's 44th Sermon, 'On the Use of Money'.

7. This can be seen from Tawney's Preface to the 1940 reprint of Gore's 1920 Essex Hall Lecture, *Christianity Applied to the Life of Men and Nations*.

8. Eliot was influenced by Demant, who had been developing his ideas long before 1949.

9. The Guild Socialists of the early twentieth century were also suspicious of the state, and they influenced Tawney (for a time) and also Demant. They usefully explored what is in the end a blind alley.

10. The GNP is the total of capital goods, finished consumption goods, and services.

11. I say 'former' because after a lapse of some years it has now been revived in a somewhat different form.

12. This is a point which seems to be assumed as self-evident, and not needing to be argued, by the Latin American liberation theologians today.

13. Marx held that capitalism must do its work before socialism is possible.

14. Though Weber wrote in 1905, the English translation by Talcott Parsons, *The Protestant Ethic and the Spirit of Capitalism*, did not appear until 1930. Tawney wrote a Foreword to it, and in 1937 he added to the Pelican edition of *Religion and the Rise of Capitalism* a new Preface which was largely concerned with Weber's thesis.

15. The chapter by Robert Moore in *Max Weber and Modern Sociology*, ed. A. Sahey, 1971.

16. See, for instance, the discussions by E. P. Thompson, *The Making of the English Working Class*, 1963, with the postscript in the Pelican edition of 1968, and E. Hobsbaum, *Labouring Man*, 1964. The case is plausible, but requires much more detailed evidence before it can be said to be established.

17. In the Third/Fourth Worlds as agricultural techniques improve, with a decreased need of workers on the land, there is a catastrophic migration to the towns.

18. Cf. Charles Elliott, *Inflation and the Compromised Church*, 1975.

2. *Ambiguities in Capitalism and Socialism Today*

1. The latest area in which promising efforts are being made is that of medical ethics.

2. I have had a special interest in this theme ever since I read Economics with Modern Economic History as a first degree at the London School of Economics, where I was a pupil of R. H. Tawney, something for which I have never ceased to be grateful.

3. Before deciding to back a 'crank' however, one needs to understand the orthodoxy which the crank is disputing. The mistake of those Christians who backed Social Credit theories was that none of them had studied economics so that they did not know what they were rejecting.

4. See above, pp. 7f.

5. 'Ideal types' is a term introduced into sociology by Max Weber. Social phenomena are so varied and fluid that structures and institutions never appear in a 'pure' form and in his view are best studied when their characteristics are viewed in an extreme form; hence ideal type.

6. In Marxist terminology the phenomenon is known as alienation.

7. There has been a revival of interest in Hayek as part of a right-wing revival, though his basic position, as will be evident from what follows, is in fact alien to most of those with right-wing opinions. Indeed so few do accept it that it might be said of him as it was said of the Stoic thinkers that he is a professor without classes. A further book appeared in 1978, *New Studies in Philosophy; Politics and the History of Ideas*.

8. As this lecture was first drafted in August 1977 an excellent example of the necessary vigilance of the state against abuses came to light in a report of the Office of Fair Trading on ready-made concrete suppliers. It showed that regular price fixing meetings had taken place between big firms in this industry, either in public houses or the houses of directors, to ensure that no one bid below the firm chosen to win a particular tender, and also to undercut outsiders when it was necessary to keep business within the ring. It is interesting to note what tender treatment we give to industry in these respects. A High Court ruling in 1969 forbids the Office of Fair Trading formally to ask companies whether they operate cartels unless it can already prove that they do; and in any case the Restrictive Practices Court can only issue an *admonition* to desist from any such practice. It is true that a civil action might be brought by someone who has suffered by the practice, but none has yet been brought. Surely the lack of registration of restrictive agreements

should be a criminal offence. At present it seems to be a risk well worth taking. A similar situation arises in the question of pollution of rivers. The Pollution Act of 1961 obliges industry to give River Boards full details of what is in its waste and in what quantities, but it does not allow the River Board to pass the information on to anyone else on the grounds of industrial secrecy.

9. This is effectively brought out in relation to the problem of developing the Third and Fourth Worlds by Sir W. Arthur Lewis in *The Evolution of the International Economic Order*, 1978. See also J. S. Singh, *A New International Order*, 1977.

10. This underlines the importance of the Habitat Conference in Vancouver in 1976, which called for supplies of clean water all over the earth by 1990.

11. It is possible that developments in micro-circuits and other factors may lead to a reversal of this tendency and to greater decentralization.

12. Other relevant statistics can be found in the *Report on the Census of Production* issued annually by HMSO (about five years after the year in question). See also S. Aaronovitch and M. C. Sawyer, *Big Business*, 1975.

13. The differences between the figures quoted here and on p. 124 (5.4% in the amount of wealth owned by the top 1% and 3.7% in the case of the top 5%) reflect the problems of detailed analysis, but do not affect the point, which is the extent of the inequalities revealed. Detailed reflection on inequalities of income and wealth is being provided by Professor A. B. Atkinson in a series of works, e.g. (with A. J. Harrison) *The Personal Distribution of Income*, 1976; for a brief treatment compare Lady Wootton's Fabian Society Tract, *In Pursuit of Equality*, 1976.

14. The second is *Mankind at the Turning Point*, 1975, the third *Reshaping the International Order*, 1977, and the fourth *Goals for Mankind*, 1977.

15. His death early in 1978 at a comparatively young age is a grievous loss.

16. Not very different from Sweden which is nine to one.

17. An excellent study of the problems of a command economy is Alec Nove, *The Soviet Economic System*, 1977, or, more briefly, D. A. Dyker, *The Soviet Economy*, 1976.

18. I think the same holds with respect to the sociological theories which allege that there is an irreversible tendency towards the disappearance of religion because of the process of secularization (compare what was said in the first lecture).

19. The USA is economically so strong that it could with resolu-

tion be practically self-sufficient and independent of external factors, but in practice it is difficult for it to ignore the relation of the dollar to the currencies of other advanced industrial countries.

20. *Religion and the Rise of Capitalism*, p. 277.

21. A good discussion is found in Z. Kenessey, *Economic Planning*, 1978, which draws on the experience of command economies like that of Hungary as well as market economies.

3. *Christianity and a Just and Sustainable Society*

1. Often quoted as 'The Church in the Modern World'. (Text in *The Documents of Vatican II*; see Bibliography.)

2. The Department on Church and Society has been under the direction of Dr Paul Abrecht through this creative post-war period, with a minute staff. He and Dr J. H. Oldham, who was the main inspirer both of the study for the Oxford Conference and of much of the preparatory work for the first Assembly of the WCC at Amsterdam in 1948, have been the two to whom the progress of ecumenical social ethics has been chiefly due.

3. In various countries different churches have followed this method of study, for example the Board of Social Responsibility of the General Synod of the Church of England or the Division of Social Responsibility of the Methodist Church in this country.

4. *Consultation on Political Economy and Ethics*, Zurich 1978; the report is available in mimeographed form.

5. See A. Dumas, *Political Theology and the Life of the Church*, 1978.

6. This was the main reason that the Producers' Co-operatives sponsored by F. D. Maurice and his 'Christian Socialist' group in the period 1848–54 collapsed. Maurice himself drew the conclusion that the workers were not sufficiently educated to undertake such responsibilities and turned his attention to establishing the Working Men's College in Camden Town. The excellence of this initiative should not disguise the fact that both his paternalism and the failures of the Co-operatives reveal a deeper flaw in human nature than his diagnosis allowed for.

7. The Zurich report (note 4) deals uncertainly with this issue.

8. Individualism and a sense of personal responsibility-in-community are very different things.

9. There will always be a place for the routine and the customary in sustaining life, but that is not the same as the elimination or reduction of drudgery.

10. I do not know a good treatment solely devoted to the theme of Christianity and affluence. On the New Testament period there is Martin Hengel, *Property and Riches in the Early Church*, 1974.

11. In a lecture, as yet unpublished, on 'Ecology and Christian Ethics'. From the lively discussion of recent years one might select T. S. Derr, *Ecology and Human Need*, 1975; H. Montefiore (ed.), *Man and Nature*, 1975; J. A. Passmore, *Man's Responsibility for Nature*, 1974; and articles in *Zygon*, July 1977.

12. I draw mainly upon the report of the Bucharest Consultation of 1974, 'Science and Technology for Human Development: the Ambiguous Future and the Christian Hope'. It is printed in *Antici-pation* No. 19, November 1974, an occasional journal privately cir-culated by the Department on Church and Society of the World Council of Churches. Preparatory Readings for the 1979 Conference, *Faith, Science and the Future*, reached me too late to be used in revising these lectures.

13. See, for instance, *Anticipation*, nos. 20, 21, 22, 23 and 24; and from among British references, *Facing up to Nuclear Power*, edited by John Francis and Paul Abrecht (1976). One issue which arises as a result of increasingly sophisticated technological developments, not-ably in connection with nuclear energy, is that of hypotheticality. It arises in cases where the usual processes of trial and error are not possible because of the magnitude of the human enterprise. This means that all possible contingencies cannot be guarded against, and yet the effect of some of them could be so severe that we could not afford to fail. Should we embark on the construction of commercial fast-breeder reactors? What do the traditional virtues of prudence and proportion say about such questions? Do they say that we should draw back altogether from an enterprise such as this, or do they urge us to take every foreseeable precaution but not rule out altogether the possibility of going ahead if the urgency of the need in terms of practicable alternatives is serious enough? My present judg-ment is not to rule such developments out, but to require that much more effort be put into considering alternatives. What is more, I think that questions such as this will become more characteristic of the situation in advanced technological societies, and may be an aspect of the 'man come of age' situation of which Bonhoeffer wrote.

14. As I understand it, it has been known for some time that burn-ing fossil fuels such as oil and coal releases carbon dioxide and that the amount in the atmosphere is increasing. It has been assumed that this raises the earth's temperature, especially at the poles, and thus creates the danger of flooding. But the amount of carbon di-oxide in the atmosphere has been found to be increasing at only half the rate at which fossil fuels are releasing it. Where has the rest gone? Not to plants, because on balance they release more than they absorb. The sea? On the other hand a study of hot and (relatively)

cold sun spots indicates that the weather should be getting colder. Is
the warming effect of the carbon dioxide counterbalancing the cool-
ing effect of the sun? The result would then be 'as you were'.
Climatology seems in much too uncertain a state for economic
policies to be based on it.

15. Intermediate Technology, as pioneered by the late E. F.
Schumacher, has much to offer less developed countries, but 'small is
beautiful' can easily be over-stated as a generalization about economic life or as an over-all philosophy.

16. See the Zurich Report (note 4) above.

17. Ocean, air and river currents do not respect national boundaries; then we must consider the sea bed; also the whole web of
links which modern transport and communications weave around us.

18. The collapse looked much more probable in the 1930s when
it did seem that the Marxist version of the inherent contradictions in
capitalism was broadly correct. But we now know not only that the
market economy in its various forms is much tougher than was
thought, but that it has had an unprecedentedly successful twenty-five
years or more until the check in the early 1970's. Indeed even in the
period 1973–77 the rate of growth in the Gross Domestic Product of
the rich countries grew by an average of 2% p.a. and that of the less
developed countries by an average of 4% p.a. (Annual Report of
GATT – the General Agreement on Tariffs and Trade, 1978). In the
same period the average rate of growth of exports in manufactured
goods from the rich countries to the less developed countries increased from 7% to 12%, and even to the non-oil-producing ones it
increased by 5%. An isolationist, protectionist policy by the rich is
possible, because of their relative wealth, but it would do economic harm to them, and much more harm to the less developed
countries.

19. What is expected from such groups is surprisingly like what is
going on in China, at least in so far as one can find out what is going
on in China. I could easily be wrong, since I have no special sources
of information, but it seems that on a secular basis the Chinese are
achieving a subordination of the individual to the group, and a
search for group harmony and consensus, which goes with a communal self-discipline and a sense of togetherness which are very
congenial to Christian thinking. The Chinese appear to show
frugality together with vitality, but not to be so tainted with the
more gross signs of consumerism that we in the West exhibit. There
are obvious possibilities of danger in this, and a Christian critique
should be alert to them, but as against our still rather strongly
individualistic attitudes in the West there seems to be a great deal in

what China is doing which is congenial to Christian thinking. Will it persist with increasing industrialization and all that goes with it?

20. The history of recent government policies of wage restraint suggests that we have two contradictory tendencies at work. (i) Differentials are more of a problem than general wage restraints; people are more sensitive to those with whom they more closely compare themselves than to the general wage level. This is partly a matter of status and power, as well as income, but not entirely, for status can sometimes be almost an inverse of pay (e.g. nurses). (ii) An equalitarian stress, partly due to concern for the lower paid, but even more to the desire of all for positional goods (cf. Hirsch, *The Social Limits to Growth*). It is naive to suppose that these are only the problems of a market economy, but we have to deal with them in the form we experience them. One could wish for more thought in the Labour movement on the matter.

21. It was carried out by Dr Kenneth Medhurst and Dr George Moyser of the Department of Government in the University of Manchester, and published under the title 'The Political Organisation of the Middle Class: the Case of the Church of England' in *Papers in Religion and Politics* (Summer Term 1977), a termly paper circulated among staff and students in the Faculty of Theology and the Department of Government, in connection with the joint degree in Religious Studies and Politics. The other survey is D. E. Butler and D. E. Stokes, *Political Change in Britain*, 1969.

22. 'Individual' suggests a replaceable unit, 'person' what is unique. Also one is only a person in a community of persons. See J. Maritain, *The Person and the Common Good*, 1948.

23. Capitalist criticisms of socialism as woolly idealism, on the grounds that people cannot be trusted and need more coercive social structures, imply also that no one can be trusted to use coercive power over others without check, a conclusion which is not usually drawn. It is to avoid this problem that the libertarian Radical wants to settle as many things as possible by automatic mechanisms, not realizing how limited (though valuable) they are. Compare the discussion in the second lecture.

24. The reason, in brief, is that in theory wages, the price level and full employment are three interlinked variables. If the first of the three can never be reduced in monetary terms the other two must be co-ordinated with it in some way; otherwise the Keynesian remedy will lead in the end to an unacceptable inflation, and a monetarist remedy to unacceptable social tensions. (The other variable is profits, and it is too small a percentage of the whole to take all the weight of adjustments.)

25. The most plausible form of the Marxist theory was worked out by Trotsky specifically to show that revolution was possible in an economically backward country (like Russia) sooner than in advanced capitalist countries.

4. *Capitalism, Socialism, Personal Freedom and Individualism*

1. This essay bears a distant resemblance to a lecture given on behalf of the Faculty of Divinity in the University of Cambridge in February 1977 with the title 'Capitalism, Socialism and Personal Freedom'.

2. In brief, 'hard' and 'soft' determinism can be differentiated. The former holds that no one could ever do anything different from what he does; the latter that the boundaries of constraint are hard to draw with precision, e.g. the extent of the influence of conditioning factors.

3. The changes in theological climate have not undermined the solid worth of L. S. Thornton's fine study, *The Common Life in the Body of Christ*, 1941.

4. The fundamental affirmation of Moral Theology, *conscientia semper sequenda* (conscience must always be followed), is an affirmation of ultimate personal worth and responsibility.

5. Cf. once more Richard Niebuhr's *Christ and Culture*.

6. Cf. the first and second Maurice Lectures.

7. In practice Puritan thought, even that of the Levellers, excluded wage-earners and alms-takers from the category of 'person'; it was the independent self-employed it had in mind.

8. Cf. the Maurice Lectures, especially the first and third.

9. C. B. Macpherson, *The Political Theory of Possessive Individualism*, 1962, especially pp. 263ff. and 270.

10. Cf. Derek Wright, *The Psychology of Moral Behaviour*, 1971.

11. John Rawls, *A Theory of Justice*, 1972; cf. the third Maurice Lecture. See also R. Nozick, *Anarchy, State and Utopia*, 1974. Rawls has received a perceptive critique from a radical corporate view in Brian Barry, *The Liberal Theory of Justice*, 1973.

12. The best easily available treatment of the Orders of Creation is still Emil Brunner's *The Divine Imperative*, ET 1937, Book III. The German title is *Das Gebot und die Ordnungen* (The Command and the Orders), one which significantly but rightly was thought to be unintelligible in Britain.

13. The twentieth century has invented the stateless person and is not proud of it.

14. Cf. the famous verse of Mrs Alexander's hymn 'All Things Bright and Beautiful' (1848):

The rich man in his castle,
The poor man at his gate:
God made them, high or lowly,
And ordered their estate.

There is disagreement as to whether there should be a comma after 'them' in the third line, and whether, if there is, it alters the sense.

15. D. Bonhoeffer, *Ethics*, 2nd English ed. 1971. Karl Barth, *Church Dogmatics* Vol. 3 Part 4, esp. pp. 36–45. Compare also the doctrine of the Divine Right of Kings to which the Church of England was so attached for so long, and which is embodied in the 1662 Book of Common Prayer, e.g. the prayers for the King at the beginning of the Order of Holy Communion.

16. Notably in the Encyclical *Quadragesimo Anno* (1931) of Pius XI.

17. In the Encyclical *Populorum Progressio* (1967) and the Apostolic Letters to Cardinal Roy, *Octogesima Adveniens* (1971).

18. Roots of this can also be found in the eighteenth century; see J. L. Talmon, *The Origins of Totalitarian Democracy*, 1952.

19. The Report of the WCC Zurich Consultation on Political Economy and Ethics (1976), referred to in the third Maurice Lecture, shows signs of this tendency.

20. The Bullock Report on Industrial Democracy (1977).

21. Those who criticize it tend to forget the hopelessly inadequate medical attention and the anxiety over doctors' bills prior to 1947. Its success has created an unrealistic level of expectation.

22. Cf. the Maurice Lectures *passim*.

5. R. H. Tawney as a Christian Moralist

1. This paper was originally given to the Manson Society in the Faculty of Theology in the University of Manchester and, slightly revised, appeared in three parts in *Theology*, April, May and June 1966. It should have included a reference to T. S. Ashton's appraisal of Tawney in the *Proceedings of the British Association* for 1962. Since 1966 three important books have appeared: in 1972 *R. H. Tawney's Commonplace Book*, which covers the years 1912–14, edited with an Introduction by J. M. Winter and the late D. M. Joslin; in 1973 *R. H. Tawney and His Times: Socialism as Fellowship*, by Dr Ross Terrill of Harvard University; and in 1978 *History and Society*, ten essays by Tawney edited with a suggestive essay on 'Tawney as a Historian' by J. M. Winter. A further volume of essays (on labour history) is planned. (There is a slight and amusing sketch of the Tawneys in A. J. Toynbee's *Acquaintances*, 1967.) Every character study emphasizes Tawney's genuine humility. It is necessary to add the word 'genuine', because humility is a virtue peculiarly liable

to internal corruption. It was Christianity which turned it in the ancient world from a vice into a virtue, and it is clear that his Christian faith is the key to Tawney's life and thought. This is not fully appreciated by those who have written about him; and his biography remains to be written. Terrill's book is the nearest to one. Dr John Atherton has dealt with Tawney more adequately in an M.A. Thesis at Manchester University in 1974, 'Moral-Theological aspects of the work of R. H. Tawney; a study of Principle applied to Property and Industry, with particular reference to *The Acquisitive Society*'. He has followed this with a detailed analysis of the whole of Tawney's life and thought in a Ph.D. Thesis in 1978, 'R. H. Tawney as a Christian Social Moralist'.

2. Some of the details of Tawney's life come from a privately cir-culated pamphlet in commemoration of his eightieth birthday, en-titled 'R. H. Tawney: a Portrait by Several Hands'; the contributors were J. R. Williams, R. Titmuss and F. J. Fisher. There is a slight sketch of him in V. P. Mehta, *Fly and the Fly-Bottle*, 1965, 170–8.

3. Out of them came a report, *Oxford and Working Class Education*, largely the work of Tawney and Alfred Zimmern.

4. H. H. Henson, *Retrospect of an Unimportant Life*, 1942, I, p. 318.

5. He played some part in the development of Trade Boards, which were concerned with fixing minimum standards in sweated trades where union organization was weak. He was a member of the Chain Trade Board from 1919 to 1922. He published studies in the establishment of minimum rates in the chain-making industry in 1914 and the tailoring industry in 1915.

6. The controversy has stimulated investigations of the develop-ment of Scholastic teaching on usury, e.g. B. W. Dempsey, *Interest and Usury*, 1948, and J. T. Noonan, *The Scholastic Analysis of Usury*, 1957.

7. Recent examples of the continuing discussion are N. Hansen, 'The Protestant Ethic as a General Condition for Economic Develop-ment', *Canadian Journal of Economic and Political Science*, November 1963; various writings of Christopher Hill, e.g. the chapter on 'Protestantism and the Rise of Capitalism' in *Essays in the Economic and Social History of Tudor and Stuart England*, 1961, and *Society and Puritanism in pre-Revolutionary England*, 1964; *The Religious Factor*, by Gerhard Lensky, 1961; the appendix to H. F. R. Catherwood, *The Christian in Industrial Society*, 1964.

8. Another way of putting this is to distinguish between seculariza-tion (a theologically necessary step in human history) and secularism (a false 'philosophy' which has tended to go with it).

9. It had originated as a Fabian Society pamphlet in 1919, *The Sickness of an Acquisitive Society*.

10. *The Acquisitive Society*, p. 239.

11. Gore, *The Sermon on the Mount*, p. 3.

12. *The Acquisitive Society*, p. 165.

13. Ibid., p. 125.

14. *The Radical Tradition*, p. 112.

15. Tawney recognized this (cf. *Equality*, pp. 69f.) but did not elaborate it.

16. This is one reason why it is hard to see how workers can efficiently control such things as price, output, sales, investment and profit policies of their firm.

17. Cf. *Religion and Social Conflict*, ed. Robert Lee and Martin Marty, 1964.

18. Quoted by H. M. Waddams, *A New Introduction to Moral Theology*, rev. ed., 1965, p. 21.

19. Daniel Jenkins, *Equality and Excellence*, 1961, p. 208.

20. Cf. Michael Young, *The Rise of the Meritocracy*, 1958.

21. Cf. *The Attack*, pp. 190ff.; *The Radical Tradition*, p. 178.

22. Walter Lippmann, *Men of Destiny*, Macmillan, New York 1927, pp. 49f., quoted by Jenkins, *Equality and Excellence*, p. 21.

23. Walter James, *The Christian in Politics*, 1962, pp. 129ff. It is noteworthy that Tawney is never referred to.

24. George Orwell, *Animal Farm*, 1945.

25. Cf. Douglas Jay, *Socialism in the New Society*, 1962, Part 4.

26. Cf. *The Economist*, 20 March 1965, p. 1243.

27. *The Radical Tradition*, p. 168.

28. *The Attack*, p. 170.

29. Ibid., p. 163.

30. Ibid., p. 92.

31. *The Radical Tradition*, p. 177.

32. *The Attack*, p. 54.

33. Ibid., p. 190.

34. Cf. ibid., pp. 191ff.

35. Ibid., p. 95.

36. Cf. the essay by Reinhold Niebuhr in *Goals of Economic Life*, ed. A. Dudley Ward, 1953, pp. 442–9.

37. It is interesting to note that Temple does not include equality among his brief list of derivative Christian Social Principles in his book.

38. The growth of the very large companies (like ICI) is one of the outstanding features of developed economies and has gone furthest in the USA. In that country, through interlocking directorates, a few hundred people have more economic – and therefore indirectly political – power than ever before in history. It can be argued that

this is used responsibly, partly because of the moral standards of those involved, partly by community checks through public opinion and the law of the state, and partly by the many power checks that a large company has within itself. It may be so, but it is hard to know whether it is so, and it remains a key point of public – and socialist – vigilance.

39. An instance of the need for central direction to grow is Town Planning. We shall never achieve decent city life without much more rigorous public control of land.

40. Article in *The Christian Century*, 7 October 1942; cf. *Christianity and Social Order*, p. 57.

41. Cf. J. K. Galbraith, *The Affluent Society*, 1958.

42. Bonhoeffer, *Ethics*, 2nd ed., 1971, Part I ch. IV, pp. 103ff.

6. *The Scene in Christian Social Ethics*

1. The substance of this essay was given in a lecture to the Annual Conference of The Modern Churchman's Union in the summer of 1977 under the title 'Whither Social Ethics?', and was subsequently published in *The Modern Churchman*, vol. XXI, Nos. 2–3, Summer 1978, pp. 81–95.

2. See above, ch. 1 note 5 and p. 147.

3. In a Tax Credit scheme, if the credits claimed exceed one's income the state supplements it to the credit level; if one's income exceeds the credits claim, one pays tax on the income above the credit line. The scheme links taxation with social security and it can be index linked. It would take about five years to work out. The Conservatives proposed a scheme in 1971 which would have distributed more to the rich than the poor because they were determined that no one should be worse off after the scheme was introduced. But if the poorer are to receive better benefits the relatively better off must pay more. The Conservatives modified their scheme rather hurriedly before the 1974 election, but without thinking it out sufficiently. Both major parties seem to have remained silent about a Tax Credit scheme since then.

4. E. Brunner, *The Divine Imperative*, ET 1937, and *Justice and the Social Order*, ET 1945; A. Nygren, *Agape and Eros*, rev. ET 1953; J. Fletcher, *Situation Ethics*, 1966.

7. *Reflections on Theologies of Social Change*

1. Some of this essay was originally part of a public lecture given for the Board of the Faculty of Divinity in the University of Cam-

bridge in November 1972, but it has been considerably rewritten and extended. The most convenient survey of the theologies discussed is to be found in *A Reader in Political Theology*, ed. Alistair Kee, 1974. See also Paul Lehmann, *The Transfiguration of Politics*, 1975.

2. Rubem Alves, 'The Dialectics of Freedom', in *A Reader in Political Theology*, pp. 35–41, reprinted from *A Theology of Human Hope*, World Publishing Co. 1970.

3. Gustavo Gutierrez, *A Theology of Liberation*, ET 1974, pp. 153–60.

4. Jürgen Moltmann, 'The Christian Theology of Hope and its Bearing on Development', *In Search of a Theology of Development*, A Sodepax Report, 1970, pp. 97–9.

5. See Isa. 10.5ff.; 44.8; 45.1; Jer. 25.9; 27.6.

Bibliography

S. Aaronovitch and M. C. Sawyer, *Big Business*, Macmillan 1975

A. B. Atkinson, *Personal Distribution of Incomes*, Allen & Unwin for the Royal Economic Society and Westview Press, Boulder, Colorado 1976

– – *The Economics of Inequality*, Clarendon Press 1975

Brian Barry, *The Liberal Theory of Justice*, Clarendon Press 1973

Karl Barth, *Church Dogmatics* 3/4, ET T. & T. Clark and Eerdmans 1961

G. Becker, *The Economic Approach to Human Behaviour*, University of Chicago Press 1977

John Bennett and others, *Christian Values and Economic Life*, Harper & Bros. 1953

A Blueprint for Survival, report commissioned by *The Ecologist*, Penguin Books 1972, revised 1977

Dietrich Bonhoeffer, *Ethics*, ET, 2nd rearranged ed., SCM Press and Macmillan, New York 1971

— *Letters and Papers from Prison*, 3rd ed. revised and enlarged, SCM Press and Macmillan 1971

Emil Brunner, *The Divine Imperative*, ET Lutterworth 1936, Macmillan, New York 1937
— *Justice and the Social Order*, ET Lutterworth and Harper & Bros. 1945
A. Bullock (chairman), *Industrial Democracy: Committee of Inquiry Report*, HMSO 1977
D. E. Butler and D. E. Stokes, *Political Change in Britain*, Macmillan 1969
H. F. R. Catherwood, *The Christian in Industrial Society*, Inter-Varsity Fellowship 1964
O. Chadwick, *The Secularisation of the European Mind in the Nineteenth Century*, Cambridge University Press 1975
Christianity and the Social Revolution, by John Lewis, Karl Polanyi and others, Victor Gollancz and Scribner's 1935
Club of Rome, *Limits to Growth* by D. H. Meadows and others, New American Library and Angus & Robertson 1972
— *Mankind at the Turning Point* by M. D. Mesarovic and others, Hutchinson and Reader's Digest Press 1975
— *Reshaping the International Order*, ed. J. Tinbergen, Hutchinson and New American Library 1977
— *Goals for Mankind*, ed. E. Lazlo, Hutchinson and New American Library 1977
Conferences: see ch. 1 note 3, ch. 3 notes 1, 2, 4 and 12
V. A. Demant, *Religion and the Decline of Capitalism*, Faber & Faber and Scribner's 1952
B. W. Dempsey, *Interest and Usury*, Dennis Dobson 1948
T. S. Derr, *Ecology and Human Need*, Westminster Press, Philadelphia 1975
The Documents of Vatican II, ed. Walter M. Abbott, SJ, Association Press, New York, and Geoffrey Chapman 1966
A. Dumas, *Political Theology and the Life of the Church*, SCM Press 1978
D. A. Dyker, *The Soviet Economy*, Granada and Macmillan, New York 1976
T. S. Eliot, *The Idea of a Christian Society*, Faber & Faber and Harcourt, Brace 1939
Charles Elliott, *Inflation and the Compromised Church*, Christian Journals, Belfast 1975
F. J. Fisher (ed.), *Essays on the Economic and Social History of Tudor and Stuart England in honour of R. H. Tawney*, Cambridge University Press 1961
Joseph Fletcher, *Situation Ethics*, SCM Press and Westminster Press 1966
— (ed.), *Christianity and Property*, Westminster Press 1948
J. Francis and Paul Abrecht (eds.), *Facing up to Nuclear Power*, St Andrew Press 1976

Milton Friedman, *Capitalism and Freedom*, University of Chicago Press 1962

J. K. Galbraith, *The Affluent Society*, Hamish Hamilton and Houghton, Mifflin, Boston 1958

A. D. Gilbert, *Religion and Society in Industrial England: Church, Chapel and Social Change 1740–1914*, Longmans 1976

Charles Gore, *The Sermon on the Mount*, John Murray 1896, Scribner's 1897

— *Christianity Applied to the Life of Men and Nations* (1920), John Murray and Musson, Toronto 1940

— and others *Property: its Duties and Rights*, Macmillan 1913

Gutierrez, Gustavo, *A Theology of Liberation*, ET Orbis Books, Maryknoll, New York 1973, SCM Press 1974

E. Halévy, *History of the English People in 1815*, ET Allen & Unwin and Harcourt, Brace 1924

F. A. von Hayek, *The Road to Serfdom*, Routledge 1944

— *Law, Legislation and Liberty: Rules and Order*, and *The Mirage of Social Justice*, Routledge & Kegan Paul and University of Chicago Press 1973 and 1976

— *New Studies in Philosophy: Politics and the History of Ideas*, Routledge & Kegan Paul 1978

M. Hengel, *Property and Riches in the Early Church*, SCM Press and Fortress Press 1974

H. Hensley Henson, *Retrospect of an Unimportant Life*, Oxford University Press 1942

Christopher Hill, *Society and Puritanism in pre-Revolutionary England*, Secker & Warburg 1964, Schocken Books, New York 1967

F. Hirsch, *The Social Limits to Growth*, Routledge & Kegan Paul and Harvard University Press 1977

E. Hobsbaum, *Labouring Man*, Weidenfeld & Nicolson 1964, Basic Books, New York 1965

Douglas Jay, *Socialism in the New Society*, Longmans 1962

Daniel Jenkins, *Equality and Excellence*, SCM Press for Christian Frontier Council 1961

Herman Kahn and A. J. Weiner, *The Year 2000*, Macmillan, New York 1968

Alistair Kee (ed.), *A Reader in Political Theology*, SCM Press and Westminster Press 1975

Z. Kenessey, *Economic Planning*, Columbia University Press 1978

F. H. Knight and T. W. Merriam, *The Economic Order and Religion*, Harper & Bros. 1945, Routledge 1948

Robert Lee and Martin Marty (eds.), *Religion and Social Conflict*, Oxford University Press, New York 1964

Paul Lehmann, *The Transfiguration of Politics*, SCM Press and Harper & Row 1975

Gerhard Lensky, *The Religious Factor*, Doubleday 1961

John Lewis, Karl Polanyi and others, *Christianity and the Social Revolution*, Gollancz 1935

W. A. Lewis, *The Evolution of the International Economic Order* Princeton University Press 1973

G. Lewy, *Religion and Revolution*, Oxford University Press 1974

Limits to Growth, see Club of Rome

A. D. Lindsay, *Christianity and Economics*, Macmillan 1933

C. B. Macpherson, *The Political Theory of Possessive Individualism*, Oxford University Press 1962

Karl Mannheim, *Ideology and Utopia*, ET Kegan Paul, Trench, Trubner and Harcourt, Brace 1936

Jacques Maritain, *True Humanism*, ET Geoffrey Bles and Scribner's 1938.

— *The Person and the Common Good*, ET Geoffrey Bles and Scribner's 1947

F. D. Maurice, *The Kingdom of Christ* (1837), reprinted James Clarke & Co. 1960

V. P. Mehta, *Fly in the Fly-Bottle*,Weidenfeld & Nicolson and Little & Ives, New York 1963, quoted from Penguin Books 1965

Hugh Montefiore (ed.), *Man and Nature*, Collins 1975

Denys Munby, *Christianity and Economic Problems*, Macmillan 1956

— *God and the Rich Society*, Oxford University Press 1961

— (ed.), *Economic Development in World Perspective*, SCM Press and Association Press 1966

National Institute of Economic and Social Research, *Poverty and Progress in Britain 1953–1973*, Cambridge University Press 1977

H. Richard Niebuhr, *Christ and Culture*, Harper & Bros. 1951, Faber & Faber 1952

Reinhold Niebuhr, *Moral Man and Immoral Society*, Scribner's 1932, SCM Press 1952

— *The Irony of American History*, Scribner's and Nisbet 1952

J. T. Noonan, *The Scholastic Analysis of Usury*, Harvard University Press 1957, Oxford University Press 1958

A. Nove, *The Soviet Economic System*, Allen & Unwin 1977

R. Nozick, *Anarchy, State and Utopia*, Basic Books, New York 1974, Blackwell, 1975

A. Nygren, *Agape and Eros*, ET, rev. ed., SPCK and Westminster Press 1953

J. H. Oldham (ed.), *The Churches Survey Their Task*, Report of the

Oxford Ecumenical Conference on Church, Community and State, Allen & Unwin and Willett, Clark & Co., Chicago 1937

George Orwell, *Animal Farm*, Secker & Warburg 1945, Harcourt, Brace 1946, Penguin Books 1951

J. A. Passmore, *Man's Responsibility for Nature*, Duckworth and Scribner's 1974

Karl Rahner, *The Shape of the Church to Come*, ET SPCK and Seabury Press 1974

Angelo Rappoport, *Dictionary of Socialism*, Allen & Unwin 1924

A. Sahey (ed.), *Max Weber and Modern Sociology*, Routledge & Kegan Paul 1971

K. Samuelsson, *Religion and Economic Action*, ET Heinemann and Basic Books, New York 1961.

E. F. Schumacher, *Small is Beautiful*, Blond & Briggs, London, and Harper & Row 1973

J. S. Singh, *A New International Order*, Praeger 1977

John Sleeman, *Basic Economic Problems*, SCM Press and Allenson, Nape ville, 1953

— *Economic Crisis: a Christian Perspective*, SCM Press and Allenson 1976

Adam Smith, *The Wealth of Nations* (1776), Penguin Books 1970

Sodepax Report, *In Search of a Theology of Development*, World Counsil of Churches, Geneva 1970

Josiah Stamp, *The Christian Ethic as an Economic Factor*, Epworth Press 1926

— *Motive and Method in a Christian Order*, Epworth Press and Abingdon Press, New York 1936

— *Christianity and Economics*, Macmillan 1939

J. L. Talmon, *The Origins of Totalitarian Democracy*, Secker & Warburg (= *The Rise of Totalitarian Democracy*, Beacon Press, New York) 1952

R. H. Tawney, *The Agrarian Problem in the Sixteenth Century*, Longmans 1912

— *The Acquisitive Society*, Harcourt, Brace 1920, George Bell 1921

— *Religion and the Rise of Capitalism*, John Murray and Harcourt, Brace 1926; Penguin Books 1938 (from which it is quoted)

— *Equality*, Allen & Unwin and Harcourt, Brace 1931; quoted from the 4th ed. revised, with a new introduction by R. M. Titmuss, Allen & Unwin 1964, Barnes & Noble 1965

— *Land and Labour in China*, Allen & Unwin and Harcourt, Brace 1932

— *The Attack and Other Papers*, Allen & Unwin and Harcourt, Brace 1953

— *Business and Politics under James I*, Cambridge University Press 1958

— *The Radical Tradition*, Allen & Unwin and Pantheon Books, New York 1964
— *History and Society*, edited with an introduction by J. M. Winter, Routledge & Kegan Paul 1978
— Historical Introduction to *Wilson's Discourse Upon Usury* (1572), George Bell and Harcourt, Brace 1925
— A. E. Bland and P. A. Brown, *English Economic History: Selected Documents*, George Bell and Macmillan, New York 1915
— and Eileen Power, *Tudor Economic Documents*, 3 vols., Longmans 1924
— *R. H. Tawney's Commplace Book*, ed. J. M. Winter and D. M. Joselin, Cambridge University Press (for the Economic History Society) 1972

William Temple, *Christianity and Social Order*, Penguin Books 1942 (reissued with Introduction by Ronald Preston, Shepheard-Walwyn and SPCK and Seabury Press 1976)

Ross Terrill, *R. H. Tawney and His Times: Socialism as Fellowship*, André Deutsch 1974

E. P. Thompson, *The Making of the English Working Class*, Victor Gollancz and Random House 1963, Penguin Books 1968

L. S. Thornton, *The Common Life in the Body of Christ*, Dacre Press 1942

Ernst Troeltsch, *The Social Teaching of the Christian Churches*, ET Allen & Unwin and Macmillan, New York 1931

Herbert Waddams, *A New Introduction to Moral Theology*, rev. ed. SCM Press and Seabury Press 1965

A. Dudley Ward (ed.), *Goals of Economic Life*, Harper & Bros. and Hamish Hamilton 1953

Max Weber, *The Protestant Ethic and the Spirit of Capitalism* (1905), ET Allen & Unwin and Scribner's 1930

Bryan Wilson, *Religion in Secular Society*, Watts, London 1966
— *Contemporary Transformations of Religion*, Oxford University Press 1976

J. Philip Wogaman, *Christians and the Great Economic Debate*, SCM Press and Westminster Press 1977

Derek Wright, *The Pyschology of Moral Behaviour*, Pnguein Books 1971

Michael Young, *The Rise of the Meritocracy*, Thames & Hudson 1958, Random House, Toronto 1959, Penguin Books 1961

Index of Names